TOP 10

Great Grammar for Great Writing

TOP 10

Great Grammar for Great Writing

Keith S. Folse
University of Central Florida

Elena Vestri Solomon
University of Nevada—Las Vegas

Donna M. Tortorella

NATIONAL GEOGRAPHIC LEARNING | HEINLE CENGAGE Learning·

Australia • Brazil • Japan • Korea • Mexico • Singapore • Spain • United Kingdom • United States

Top 10: Great Grammar for Great Writing
Keith S. Folse, Elena Vestri Solomon,
and Donna M. Tortorella

Editorial Director: Joe Dougherty

Publisher: Sherrise Roehr

Acquisitions Editor, Academic ESL: Tom Jefferies

VP, Director of Content Development: Anita
Raducanu

Director of Product Marketing: Amy Mabley

Director of Global Field Marketing: Ian Martin

Executive Marketing Manager: Jim McDonough

Senior Field Marketing Manager: Donna Lee
Kennedy

Product Marketing Manager: Katie Kelley

Development Editor: Kathleen Smith

Content Project Manager: Tan Jin Hock

Print Buyer: Susan Carroll

Production Management: Matrix Productions, Inc.

Compositor: Integra

Cover Designer: Dammora Inc.

Photo Credits
p. 6: © Michael Valdez/iStockphoto; p. 38:
© Henry Lucenius/iStockphoto; p. 44:
© Kevin Russ/iStockphoto; p. 60: © Andrea
Gingerich/iStockphoto; p. 62: © iStockphoto;
p. 68 (top): © Robin Arnold/iStockphoto; p. 68
(bottom): © Graeme Purdy/iStockphoto; p. 69:
© iStockphoto; p. 76: © John Woodstock/
iStockphoto; p. 99 (left): © Ablestock/
IndexOpen; p. 99 (right): © IndexOpen; p. 118:
© photos.com; p. 129: © photolibrary.com
pty, ltd/IndexOpen; p. 134: © Mariev Rodrig/
iStockphoto; p. 138: © James Denk/IndexOpen;
p. 140: © photos.com; p. 144 (top):
© AbleStock/IndexOpen; p. 144 (bottom):
© Image D/IndexOpen; p. 158: © lillis werder/
iStockphoto; p. 161: © Tim McCaig/iStockphoto;
p. 166: © Dieter Spears/iStockphoto; p. 172:
© FogStock LLC/IndexOpen; p. 175: © FogStock
LLC/IndexOpen; p. 181: © Ethan Myerson/
iStockphoto; p. 190: © PHOTICK/IndexOpen.

For permission to use material from this text or product,
submit all requests online at **www.cengage.com/permissions**
Further permissions questions can be emailed to
permissionrequest@cengage.com

Library of Congress Control Number: 2007930775

ISBN-13: 978-0-618-48105-7

ISBN-10: 0-618-48105-2

National Geographic Learning
20 Channel Center Street
Boston, MA 02210
USA

Cengage Learning is a leading provider of customized learning solutions with
office locations around the globe, including Singapore, the United Kingdom,
Australia, Mexico, Brazil, and Japan.

Cengage Learning products are represented in Canada by Nelson Education, Ltd.

Visit National Geographic Learning online at **elt.heinle.com**

Visit our corporate website at **www.cengage.com**

Printed in the United States of America
5 6 7 8 9   19 18 17 16 15

Contents

Overview

Top 10 offers instruction and writing practice in ten essential grammar areas for better English writing. ESL writers at the intermediate level tend to produce writing with a high number of surface-level errors, especially errors in grammar. *Top 10* addresses these types of errors while working on building better sentences and paragraphs.

Because editing of student writing is a primary objective for many courses at the intermediate level, many exercises in *Top 10* deal with editing or with producing original writing followed by editing. These exercises attempt to focus students' attention on common grammatical errors and then teach students various options for making corrections.

Course and Students

Top 10 is designed for intermediate students. It contains enough material for 60 to 70 classroom hours, depending on the class level and the amount of writing and work that is completed outside of class. If time limitations exist, the material could be covered in as few as 45 hours with a faster group, provided that many of the exercises are assigned as homework.

A major obstacle to future educational plans for many students is not being able to write effectively and easily in English. Thus, the quality of any written work that they do is very important. Since grammar is often the main issue that keeps ESL students from producing a satisfactory piece of original writing, the exercises in *Top 10* focus exclusively on grammar problems that are common in writing.

The title *Top 10* refers to the ten chapters in the book. Each chapter focuses on a common area of difficulty of English grammar in student writing: parts of speech (i.e., word forms); verbs, nouns and articles; subject–verb agreement; modals; prepositions; adjectives; sentence patterns (with verbs, adjectives, and adverbs); sentence types; and common grammar errors. These ten areas were selected after surveying many experienced teachers, student writers, textbooks, and course curricula to determine the most serious and pervasive grammar problems for intermediate student writing.

Students vary, so ultimately it is you, the teacher, who is always the best judge of which chapters should be covered in which order and to what extent. No one knows the language needs of your students better than you do. It is up to you to gauge the needs of your students and then match those needs with the material in *Top 10*.

Text Organization

Each of the ten chapters focuses on one grammar area that affects the quality of student writing. Each chapter is independent of the others and can therefore be taught in any sequence.

Three appendixes appear at the back of the book: Appendix 1 lists irregular verb forms; Appendix 2 provides instruction and practice with capitalization; Appendix 3 provides instruction and practice with punctuation. We strongly recommend that teachers go over these appendixes early in the course. Students will then know where they are in the book and will be able to refer to the appendixes as needed as they do the writing activities in each chapter.

Supporting web exercises for *Top 10*, as well as the Answer Key, can be found at:

elt.heinle.com/top10

Contents of a Chapter

Following are the common features and exercise types in each chapter. While not all chapters include every feature or exercise type, these are the most common chapter components.

Grammar Reviews and Explanations

The grammar reviews and explanations have been written to focus specifically on problems that occur in student writing, not in speech. *Top 10* is not meant to be an exhaustive grammar book; it reviews common problem areas and helps students focus their attention on the gap between how they are writing and how they should be writing. Because of this, teachers may note the absence of certain grammar points. For example, in Chapter 2, "Review of Verbs," instead of covering all the verb tenses in English, we focus on six common tenses. Our analysis of student writing needs indicates that it is more prudent for intermediate ESL writers to focus their attention on these specific tenses, so we have limited our instruction and subsequent practice to just these six. (In contrast, a comprehensive grammar book would most likely provide a chart with all twelve verb tenses, including less common tenses such as future perfect progressive.)

Exercise Types

Second language acquisition (SLA) research shows the importance of awareness in the second language learning process. Students using this text have had basic grammar instruction but continue to make errors. The exercises in *Top 10* are designed to raise students' consciousness of the types of errors that they make in their writing. Additional SLA research has demonstrated the importance of the number of exercises—frequency of practice—in comparison with the nature of the exercises. Therefore, we have included multiple exercises for more difficult grammar points. However, teachers do not need to assign all of these exercises for a given grammar point if students have demonstrated mastery. Some teachers may wish to save some of these exercises for review at a later time.

Original Sentences   Some exercises ask students to write original sentences to illustrate a specific aspect of a given grammar point. We recommend that you have students discuss their answers in groups and possibly write some of their sentences on the board for general class discussion about what is correct and what is not correct, as well as why a gap between the two exists for a particular student.

Identifying Grammatical Elements   In this type of exercise, students circle or underline the target grammatical element. We believe that it is incorrect to force full production of a grammatical point initially; instead, we first want our students to be able to identify the target structure.

Selecting the Correct Form   This traditional type of exercise usually presents students with two or three answer options, and students must underline or circle the single correct answer. The incorrect answer options are almost always forms that students with various first languages would write. Thus, this kind of exercise is harder than it might appear.

Editing Exercise: Editing of Sentences   Because a paragraph is only as good as the sentences in it, this type of exercise presents students with sentences one at a time. The sentences are often about a single topic and are therefore related to each other. Students are asked to focus on one specific grammar issue, such as verb tenses, and check for that specific grammar point in each sentence.

Editing Exercise: Editing of Paragraphs   In this type of exercise, students are presented with a complete paragraph. Common topics covered include business, history, geography, sociology, hobbies, and trivia. Students are not told where the errors are, but they are always told how many or what type of errors to look for. Thus, students gain practice in editing language and in analyzing a paragraph.

These two points are important in helping students practice looking for, finding, and correcting *specific* errors that they are likely to be making. Since the teaching goal is to enable students to edit for specific kinds of errors, it makes sense to tell them what errors to look for. For example, if we want students to check for subject-verb agreement and word endings, then teachers and materials should train students to look for these specific mistakes. Instead of the more typical directions that ask students to find "the errors" in a given piece of writing, the most effective exercises direct students to find, for example, two subject-verb errors and three word ending errors, or to find five errors.

Guided Writing   In this exercise, which comes near the end of each chapter, students are given a paragraph to revise. They revise according to specific instructions that focus on grammar elements in the current chapter and other general grammar points. These grammar points reflect the exact types of self-edits that we hope our learners will develop, such as checking all verbs for subject-verb agreement or checking that no sentences are fragments.

Original Writing   In order to achieve the goal of connecting both the grammar instruction and focused review in student writing, each chapter of *Top 10* ends with an exercise called "Original Writing." Students are given a prompt to which they are asked to respond by writing one paragraph, two paragraphs, or an essay. (It is up to each teacher to establish the writing length parameters of any exercise.) We believe that students should not be writing extensively but *intensively* when the goal is improving writing accuracy. Thus, while this activity asks students to write a short piece, the grammar demands are high. Students are told to practice certain aspects of the grammar in that chapter, to underline their original examples, and to check their correctness with a partner. Underlining key linguistic features has been shown to aid in students' noticing and learning of new material.

More About the Exercises in Top 10

Teachers have long noticed that their students may do well in a grammar class where the focus is on one grammatical form in one type of exercise, but these same students may experience writing problems when trying to transfer or apply this knowledge to original writing. For some reason, students often do not transfer the material that they were just taught to their writing. As a result, the majority of the exercises in *Top 10* deal with language in a context. This includes language in a series of related sentences, in a whole paragraph, or even in a short essay. Our experience has shown that students can improve their editing for a specific kind of grammatical error when they review the grammar issue and then practice their editing skills in sentences, whole paragraphs, and essays. The over 200 exercises in *Top 10* and additional web activities offer more than enough material to satisfy most students' written grammar needs.

Acknowledgments

Top 10 is the result of the planning, input, and persistence of many people. We are especially grateful to our immediate editors at both Heinle, Cengage Learning and Houghton Mifflin, who have nurtured this project through its development. We are especially grateful to Kathy Sands-Boehmer, Joann Kozyrev, and Susan Maguire for their encouragement in the early stages of *Top 10*.

We wish to express our gratitude to Kathy Smith, our development editor, who so diligently helped us implement reviewers' suggestions into this work.

Finally, we thank other teachers and reviewers whose comments were instrumental in the development of *Top 10*: Edna Bagley, Nassau Community College; Aileen Gum, San Diego City College; Jacqueline Cunningham, Harold Washington College; Mary Corredor, Austin Community College; Kathleen Flynn, Glendale Community College; Tracy Henniger-Wiley, Lane Community College; Nancy Megarity, Collin County Community College; and Shirley Lundblade, Mt. San Antonio College.

Keith S. Folse
Elena Vestri Solomon
Donna M. Tortorella

Parts of Speech

Words have different purposes, or functions, in a sentence. In English, words are classified into different groups based on the function of the words in a sentence. These groups are called **parts of speech.**

In English, there are seven* parts of speech that are important for writing:

- verb
- noun
- pronoun
- preposition
- adjective
- adverb
- conjunction

The <u>brown</u> house <u>on</u> Wilson Street <u>has</u> three <u>bedrooms</u>.
     ADJ   PREP   VERB   NOUN

Joseph speaks <u>quickly</u>, <u>but</u> his English is good because <u>he</u> speaks very clearly.
               ADV CONJ   PRON

1.1 Verbs

A **verb** is the most important word in a sentence. A verb shows action or being (existence).

    action: take, write, run, select, show, call

    existence: be (am, is, are, was, were)

Every sentence must have a verb. Forgetting the verb is a serious error.

    Remember: No verb = No meaning

---

*Note (to teacher): Traditionally, there are eight parts of speech, including *interjections*, but interjections are not common in academic writing and therefore will not be covered here. In addition, some books treat *determiners* (some, any), *demonstratives* (this, those), and *articles* (a, the) as separate categories. In the traditional system of eight parts of speech, however, determiners, demonstratives, and articles are classified as adjectives.

Every sentence must also have a subject. The subject is the noun or pronoun that does the action of the verb.

In the following paragraph, the subject of each sentence has one line under it and the verb has two lines under it.

> My <u>name</u> <u><u>is</u></u> Keith. <u>I</u> <u><u>am</u></u> a student at Washington High School. My best <u>friend</u> <u><u>is</u></u> Joshua. <u>He</u> <u><u>lives</u></u> about two blocks from our school. His <u>family</u> <u><u>moved</u></u> here about five years ago. <u>Joshua and I</u> <u><u>are</u></u> in the eleventh grade. <u>We</u> <u><u>will graduate</u></u> next year.

A sentence that does not have a subject or a verb is called a sentence fragment.*

Fragment:	The <u>president</u> of the U.S. in the White House.
Correct:	The <u>president</u> of the U.S. <u><u>lives</u></u> in the White House.
Fragment:	<u><u>Is</u></u> very hot in New York City in July.
Correct:	<u>It</u> <u><u>is</u></u> very hot in New York City in July.

The verb in a sentence can be more than one word.

1 word:	I <u><u>cook</u></u> eggs for breakfast every morning.
2 words:	I <u><u>am cooking</u></u> scrambled eggs now.
2 words:	I <u><u>can cook</u></u> eggs with cheese and tomatoes.
2 words:	I <u><u>do</u></u> not <u><u>cook</u></u> eggs with meat.
2 words:	I <u><u>did</u></u> not <u><u>cook</u></u> eggs with meat yesterday.

A sentence can have more than one verb.

1 verb:	The assistant <u><u>answered</u></u> the phone.
2 verbs:	The assistant <u><u>answered</u></u> the phone and <u><u>wrote</u></u> a message.
3 verbs:	The assistant <u><u>answered</u></u> the phone, <u><u>wrote</u></u> a message, and <u><u>gave</u></u> it to Mary.

Sentences that are commands (imperative) do not have a written subject: *Open the door, please.* The subject (you) is understood.

Exercise 1   Read the sentences about my math class. Draw one line under the subjects and two lines under the verbs. Hint: Some sentences have more than one subject and verb. The first one has been done for you.

1. My math <u>class</u> <u><u>is</u></u> from 8:00 a.m. to 8:45 a.m. every day.

2. Our class meets in Room 218.

3. The name of the building is Margaret Cook Hall.

4. Students like Room 218.

5. Room 218 has 50 desks in it, and two long blackboards are on the walls.

---

fragment: a piece or part of something, incomplete

6. Every weekday morning I wake up at 6:30 a.m., take a shower, and then eat my breakfast before I go to my math class.

7. Students are often tired in early morning classes, but you won't see any sleepy or bored faces in this class.

8. In fact, if you want a good seat in this class, you have to arrive early.

9. I don't think that anyone arrives late to this class.

10. The math teacher's name is Dr. Wilson.

11. The name of the book that we use in this class is "Mathematics for Today."

12. Like most of my classmates, I truly enjoy this class because the teacher is so good.

13. I have never liked math very much, but I like this class with Dr. Wilson.

Exercise 2   Read the conversation between two friends who run into* each other. Draw one line under the subjects and two lines under the verbs. Hint: Some sentences have more than one verb. The first one has been done for you.

Alfredo: Hi, Barbara. How are you?

Barbara: Hey, Alfredo. I'm doing fine. I haven't seen you in a long time.

Alfredo: I know. My job takes so much of my time these days.

Barbara: Where do you work?

Alfredo: I'm a realtor. I work at Palm Property.

Barbara: That's right. I knew that! How are your parents?

Alfredo: They are doing well. My mom is helping my brother with his new house, and my dad is still working at the bank.

Barbara: Well, I hope to see them again. Maybe your family can come to my house for dinner one night. How does that sound?

Alfredo: Well, I will talk to them about it, and then I can call you.

Barbara: Great. I'm so glad that we ran into* each other. Take care.

Alfredo: Thanks, Barbara. See you.

———————

run into: meet by chance

Exercise 3   Read the sentences about mathematics. Draw one line under the subjects and two lines under the verbs. If a sentence does not have a subject and a verb, write *fragment* on the line to the left. Then add a subject or a verb that makes sense. Be sure to add your new verb in the correct place. The first two have been done for you.

$$\frac{1}{2} + \frac{2}{3} = \frac{3}{6} + \frac{4}{6} = \frac{7}{6}$$

_____ 1. In math, <u>fractions</u> <u><u>are</u></u> parts of a number.

                      are

___*fragment*___ 2. For example, $\frac{1}{2}$ and $\frac{2}{3}$ fractions.
                            ^

_____ 3. Examples of whole numbers are 4, 14, and 40.

_____ 4. Are the opposite of fractions.

_____ 5. We call the bottom number of a fraction the denominator.

_____ 6. The numerator is the top number of a fraction.

_____ 7. In the fraction $\frac{3}{4}$, 3 is the numerator, and 4 is the denominator.

_____ 8. If you want to add two fractions, they must the same denominator.

_____ 9. The problem "$\frac{1}{2} + \frac{2}{3}$" is a little difficult because the denominators of

the fractions different.

10. Write an original sentence about fractions. Underline the subject once and the verb twice.

_____

_____

Exercise 4   Read the sentences about learning English. Draw one line under the subjects and two lines under the verbs. If a sentence does not have a subject and a verb, write *fragment* on the line to the left. Then add a subject or a verb that makes sense. Be sure to add your new verb in the correct place. The first two have been done for you.

_____ 1. For some people, <u>English</u> <u><u>is</u></u> a difficult language.

__*fragment*__ 2. For other people, English ^{is} not very difficult.

_____ 3. For these people, is very easy.

_____ 4. Some parts of English more difficult than others.

_____ 5. For example, spelling and pronunciation in English are difficult.

_____ 6. In English, there many different pronunciations for one letter.

_____ 7. As a result, I can't English words very well.

_____ 8. You can spell the same sound in two or three ways.

_____ 9. Sometimes you write *ai* as in *rain*, and other times you *ay* as in *Ray*.

10. Write an original sentence about learning English. Underline the subject once and the verb twice.

_____

_____

Exercise 5   Read the sentences about cooking. Draw one line under the subjects and two lines under the verbs. If a sentence does not have a subject and a verb, write *fragment* on the line to the left. Then add a subject or a verb that makes sense. Be sure to add your new verb in the correct place. Remember that some sentences contain more than one subject and more than one verb. The first one has been done for you.

_____ 1. <u>I</u> <u><u>enjoy</u></u> cooking because <u>it</u> <u><u>relaxes</u></u> me.

_____ 2. Of course some things are hard to cook, but many common dishes

easy to prepare.

_____ 3. My favorite food scrambled eggs.

_____ 4. When you cook scrambled eggs, you

eggs, butter, and a little salt.

_____ 5. You can onions or green peppers in

egg dishes if you like vegetables.

_____ 6. The truth is that the exact list of

ingredients is up to you.

_____ 7. Another one of my favorite breakfast dishes is pancakes.

_____ 8. Cooking pancakes a little more difficult than cooking eggs.

_____ 9. If you want to make great pancakes, consult a cookbook for a variety

of delicious recipes.

10. Write an original sentence about cooking breakfast. Underline the subject once and

the verb twice.

_____

_____

Exercise 6   Read the sentences about British Columbia. Draw one line under the subjects and two lines under the verbs. If a sentence does not have a subject and a verb, write *fragment* on the line to the left. Then add a subject or a verb that makes sense. Be sure to add your new verb in the correct place. The first one has been done for you.

_____ 1. Where is British

Columbia?

_____ 2. How much information

do you know about this

great Canadian province?

_____ 3. The province of British

Columbia is located in the western part of Canada.

_____ 4. The Pacific Ocean is to the west of British Columbia, and the

province of Alberta to the east.

_____ 5. The U.S. state of Washington lies to the south, and the Yukon

Territory and the Northwest Territories are to the north.

_____ 6. This province of Canada features some of the most beautiful natural

scenery in the world.

_____ 7. For example, are mountains and lakes with beautiful green forests.

_____ 8. Approximately 4,100,000 people in British Columbia.

_____ 9. Victoria is the capital of British Columbia.

_____ 10. Many people in British Columbia because the weather is mild.

_____ 11. Unlike the rest of Canada, British Columbia mild weather.

12. Write an original sentence about British Columbia. Underline the subject once and

the verb twice.

_____

_____

Exercise 7   Choose a topic that you like. Then write six sentences about that topic. Draw two lines
under the verbs in your sentences.

Topic: _____

1. _____

_____

2. _____

_____

3. _____

_____

4. _____

_____

5. _____

_____

6. _____

_____

1.2   Nouns

A **noun** is the name of a person, place, thing, or quality.

person:	Mrs. Smith, the doctor, the boys
place:	Cairo, a hotel, a soccer stadium
thing:	chocolate ice cream, my car, a small radio
quality:	honesty, patience, love

A **proper noun** is the name of a specific person, place, or thing. A proper noun begins with a capital letter.

person:	Mrs. Smith, Bill Clinton, Indira Gandhi
place:	Cairo, the Hilton Hotel, British Columbia
thing:	Pepsi-Cola, United Airlines, Toyota

Exercise 8   Read the sentences about what my family does every summer. Circle the nouns.
Hint: The number in parentheses tells you the number of nouns in each sentence.
The first one has been done for you.

1. (3) (Summer) is my favorite (season) of the (year).

2. (5) The reason that I like summer is that my family travels to Peru every summer.

3. (5) In this picture, you can see my wife, my two children, and our new cat next to our new house.

4. (5) We took this picture in 2006 just before we went to the airport to catch our flight to Peru.

5. (3) When we go to Peru, we stay at my grandparents' house outside Lima.

6. (6) My grandmother, grandfather, and aunt live in a large house near a park with a very small lake.

7. (8) When my family arrives at my grandparents' house, all the people in the house (including my grandparents and any neighbors who are there) run out to greet us with kisses and hugs.

8. (5) One thing that I really like about our visit is that my grandmother cooks chicken with vegetables.

9. (3) My mom tries to cook this same dish, but it never has the same taste.

10. (3) The only bad part about our trip is that we only stay for two weeks, which seems very short to me.

Exercise 9 Complete these sentences with any noun that makes sense. The first one has been done for you.

1. _____Biology_____ is my favorite school subject.

2. I think that the best season of the year is _____ .

3. If I could visit any country in the world, I would like to visit _____ .

4. My favorite restaurant is _____ .

5. _____ is my favorite color.

6. My favorite food is _____ .

7. Of all my relatives, _____ is my favorite relative.

8. The person who has had the most influence on my life is _____ .

When you use the word *because* to explain a reason, your sentence needs two subjects and two verbs.

I am hungry now **because** I ate only an apple for lunch.
1 1   2 2

A common mistake is to forget either the subject or the verb after *because*.

Incorrect: No subject: Bolivia does not have a seafood industry because does not have a coastline.

Incorrect: No verb: The air in Mexico City is polluted because there too many cars.

Exercise 10 Below are the first four sentences from Exercise 9. Complete each sentence with a reason beginning with the word *because*. Make sure that you have a subject and a verb after the word *because*. The first one has been done for you.

1. _____Biology_____ is my favorite school subject because ____I enjoy nature.____

2. I think that the best season of the year is _____ because _____

_____

3. If I could visit any country in the world, I would like to visit _____

because _____

_____

4. My favorite restaurant is _____ because _____

_____

Exercise 11   Choose a topic that you like. (If you want, use a topic from Exercise 10.) Then write six sentences about that topic. Circle the nouns in your sentences. Use *because* in one or two of your sentences.

Topic: _____

1. _____

2. _____

3. _____

4. _____

5. _____

6. _____

1.3   Pronouns

A **pronoun** is a word that can replace or substitute for a noun.

nouns:	**Karla** drinks **black coffee** every morning.
pronouns:	**She** drinks **it** every morning. (*She* = Karla; *it* = black coffee)
nouns:	**My uncle** buys **magazines** every week.
pronouns:	**He** buys **them** every week. (*He* = My uncle; *them* = magazines)

Exercise 12   Read the paragraph about a difficult decision. Write N for noun or P for pronoun to indicate the part of speech of each underlined word. The first one has been done for you.

A Difficult Decision

       N
Kevin and Silvia Johnson have a problem. They want to select a pet for their son
  1   2   3   4   5   6

Michael. He is only seven years old. Kevin thinks that the best pet for Michael is a cat.
       7   8   9

Kevin thinks cats are good animals because they are clean. Silvia does not agree with
          10   11   12

him. She knows that Michael really likes dogs. Silvia prefers them to cats because they
13 14   15   16   17

are more emotional than cats. Both Kevin and Silvia have a difficult decision to make.
                                                         18

Kinds of Pronouns

Two kinds of pronouns are important: subject and object. Subject pronouns usually come before the verb.

> *Subject:*   I   you   he   she   it   we   they
>
> Yesterday **I** called him.
>
> Today **he** called me.

Object pronouns come after the verb.

> *Object:*   me   you   him   her   it   us   them
>
> Yesterday he called **me.**
>
> Today I called **him.**

Object pronouns also come after prepositions.

> Joy gave the books *to* **him** yesterday.
>
> Is this gift *for* **me?**
>
> Do they have their books *with* **them** now?

Exercise 13   Write a noun in the first sentence. Then use a pronoun in a second sentence to refer to that noun. Circle the pronoun. The first one has been done for you.

Nouns and Pronouns

1. Today is _____ my birthday _____ . ___ (It) is my favorite day of the year. ___

2. The capital of Japan is _____ . _____

   _____

3. My mother's name is _____ . _____

   _____

4. My name is _____ . _____

   _____

5. My friend's name is _____ . _____

   _____

6. My best friend and I like _____ . _____

   _____

1.4 Prepositions

A **preposition** is a word that shows the relationship between a noun (or pronoun) and the rest of the sentence.

Common Prepositions

about	at	for	near	on	until
above	before	from	next to	to	with
after	by	in	of	under	without

Prepositions have many purposes, but they often give us information about place, time, and direction.

place:	**in** the classroom	**on** the table	**near** the bank
	under the car	**at** the hotel	**next to** my car
time:	**in** the morning	**in** March	**in** 1985
	in ten minutes	**for** ten minutes	**at** 9:45
	on Monday	**from** noon	**until** midnight
direction:	**to** the bank	**from** the bank	

The combination of a preposition with its object (and any modifiers or describing words) is called a **prepositional phrase**.

preposition	+ modifier(s)	+ object	=	**prepositional phrase**
in	that	classroom	=	**in** that classroom
under	our old red	sofa	=	**under** our old red sofa
on	the second	floor	=	**on** the second floor

Exercise 14 Read the paragraph about a family trip. Circle the fifteen prepositions. Underline the object of each preposition. The first one has been done for you.

My Family Trip to South America

(In) 2005, my family took a trip to South America. First, we visited Colombia.

We stayed in a nice hotel in Bogota. Our hotel was near a great museum. Next, we

traveled from Colombia to Peru. In Peru, we went to Machu Pichu. It was amazing!

After Peru, we went to Argentina. I bought some great t-shirts at a small shop by the

Presidential Palace. I had a great time with my family in South America.

Exercise 15   Answer these questions with true answers about your situation. Answer in complete sentences. Circle the prepositions and underline the object of each preposition.

1. Where were you born? _____

_____

2. Where do you live? _____

_____

3. Where do you work? _____

_____

4. Do you live with your family? (If yes, name the family members. If no, write a negative

sentence.) _____

_____

5. What food can you cook or make by yourself? _____

_____

6. What kind of music do you listen to? _____

_____

1.5   Adjectives

An **adjective** is a word that describes a noun or pronoun.

adjectives: good, delicious, happy, interesting, important, serious, green, cold, many, Mexican, French, English, Chinese, difficult, clean, six

Adjectives answer the questions "Which?" "How many?" "What kind?" For example, this sentence has three adjectives:

My **white** cat sometimes eats **two** pieces of **fried** chicken.

Which cat?   *How many pieces?*   *What kind of chicken?*

In English, adjectives can come after *be* or before nouns.

after be: Canada *is* **big.**
　　　　　　　BE ADJ

before noun: Canada is a **big** *country.*
　　　　　　　　　　　　　ADJ   NOUN

after be: Elvis Presley *was* very **popular.**
　　　　　　　　　　　BE　　　ADJ

before noun: Elvis Presley was a very **popular** *singer.*
　　　　　　　　　　　　　　　　ADJ   NOUN

Exercise 16 Read the paragraph about birds. Circle the fourteen adjectives. The first one has been done for you.

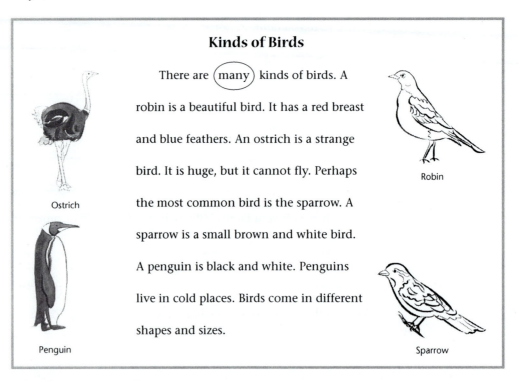

Kinds of Birds

There are (many) kinds of birds. A robin is a beautiful bird. It has a red breast and blue feathers. An ostrich is a strange bird. It is huge, but it cannot fly. Perhaps the most common bird is the sparrow. A sparrow is a small brown and white bird. A penguin is black and white. Penguins live in cold places. Birds come in different shapes and sizes.

Ostrich

Robin

Penguin

Sparrow

Exercise 17 Read these sentences about animals. Fill in each blank with any adjective that completes the sentence. The first one has been done for you.

1. Cats are _____*secretive*_____ animals.

2. Most dogs are very _____ .

3. I do not like spiders because they are _____ .

4. My favorite zoo animal is a giraffe because it is _____ .

5. Some people dislike cats because they are sometimes _____ .

6. My neighbor says that fish are the best pets because they are always

   _____ .

7. I could never keep a horse as a pet because horses are too _____ .

8. I know people who have pet rabbits because they believe that rabbits are

   _____ .

1.6   Adverbs

An **adverb** is a word that describes (modifies) a verb, an adjective, or another adverb. Adverbs tell how (manner), when, where, how often, and how much.

how:	Ostriches can run **quickly.**
when:	We saw an ostrich **yesterday.**
where:	Ostriches don't live in Canada. They can't live **there** because it is cold.
how often:	Ostriches have wings, but they **never** fly.
how much:	Ostriches can run **extremely** quickly.

Exercise 18   Read the sentences about driving. Write *yes* or *no* after each underlined word to indicate if it is an adverb. The first one has been done for you.

1. Driving on the highway can be very ___*yes*___ dangerous ___*no*___ .

2. People drive incredibly _____ fast _____ on the highway.

3. I usually _____ try to avoid _____ the highway.

4. I saw three _____ accidents on the highway recently _____ .

5. I am sure _____ that I will see another accident tomorrow _____ .

Exercise 19   Choose a topic that you like. Then use the adverbs in parentheses to write six sentences about that topic. Circle the adverbs in your sentences. In number 6, use any adverb that has not been used in this exercise.

Topic: _____

(very)   1. _____

_____

(sometimes) 2. _____

_____

(every day) 3. _____

_____

(well)   4. _____

_____

(carefully) 5. _____

_____

(   ) 6. _____

_____

1.7 Conjunctions

A **conjunction** is a word that connects parts of a sentence together.

In the middle of a sentence: *and, but, or, so*

Central America includes Nicaragua, Guatemala, **and** Honduras.

At this school, students can study Japanese **or** Chinese.

He travels for his job, **so** he is often out of town.

In the middle OR at the beginning: *because, although, when, before, after*

He speaks Spanish **because** he is from Mexico.

Because he is from Mexico, he speaks Spanish.

The car had problems **before** I bought it.

Before I bought the car, it had problems.

Exercise 20   Read the paragraph about a very famous person. Circle the twelve conjunctions. The first one has been done for you.

Lady Diana Spencer

I think one of the most important people in modern history is Princess Diana. Her full title was Lady Diana Frances Spencer. She was born in 1961. On July 29, 1981, she married Prince Charles (when) she was only 20 years old. Diana and Charles had two children, William and Harry. Because their marriage was not successful, she and Charles divorced in 1996. After Diana was divorced, she continued to work for several important charities and causes. Diana was very popular, so the paparazzi* tried to take pictures of her and her children all the time. In 1997, Diana was killed when her car crashed. Although Diana died in 1997, her memory continues to live because she was popular with so many people.

---

paparazzi: news people, press photographers

1.8 Word Forms

Sometimes you can look at a word and guess its part of speech. For example, if a word ends in *-tion* or *-ation*, it is probably a noun.

(a) The teacher's **selection** of the questions is usually good.

(b) The **action** of the police was very rapid.

(c) The teacher will give us an **examination** tomorrow.

If you want to use these three words as verbs instead of nouns, you must change the word form. The verb forms are *select, act,* and *examine.*

Incorrect: (d) The teacher ~~selections~~ good questions.

Correct: (e) The teacher **selects** good questions.

Why is (d) wrong? Why is (e) correct?

The answer is that you must use a verb form, not a noun form.

Here are four examples of useful word formation patterns:

verb + -*(a)tion* → noun   select → selection

verb + -*able* → adjective   chew → chewable

verb + -*ment* → noun   announce → announcement

adjective + -*ly* → adverb   slow → slowly

Exercise 21   Fill in the correct word form. The first one has been done for you.

verb + -*(a)tion* → noun

1. elect   _____ *election* _____

2. distribute   _____

3. vary   _____

4. complete   _____

5. hesitate   _____

6. collect   _____

verb + -*able* → adjective

7. drink   _____

8. enjoy   _____

9. like   _____

10. predict   _____

11. suit   _____

12. accept   _____

verb + -*ment* → noun

13. enjoy   _____

14. require   _____

15. agree   _____

16. move   _____

17. state   _____

18. improve   _____

adjective + -*ly* → adverb

19. quick   _____

20. careful   _____

21. cheap   _____

22. beautiful   _____

23. possible   _____

24. probable   _____

Exercise 22   Read the sentences about making a public speech. If the underlined word is the incorrect form, write a correction above. If the underlined word is correct, write C above. There are four errors.

1. An important part of <u>communication</u> is the ability to make a public speech.

2. The first task for public speakers is the <u>select</u> of the topic of their speech.

3. After they <u>selection</u> the topic, they must brainstorm ideas for the content of the speech.

4. When speakers identify ideas that are not important to the topic, they <u>eliminate</u> them.

5. When all of the speakers' ideas are on paper, they <u>organization</u> them.

6. One way that speakers <u>organize</u> their ideas is from least important to most important.

7. If you want to prepare a public speech but need some help in the process, perhaps a skillful public speaker can <u>demonstration</u> this for you.

8. In the end, you too can <u>enjoy</u> speaking in public.

■ GUIDED WRITING

Exercise 23   Read the paragraph. Then rewrite it by making the ten changes listed. Careful! You may have to make other changes.

1. Change *English* to *French.*
2. Change *vocabulary* to *words* and make necessary changes.
3. Add *incredibly* before *difficult for me to pronounce.*
4. Add *a lot of* before *problems with the sounds of B and V.*
5. Change *B and V* to *R* and make necessary changes.
6. Connect the last two sentences with *and.* (Be sure to add the correct punctuation.)
7. Add *in two areas* to the first sentence in the most logical place.
8. Begin the eighth sentence with the word *most.*
9. Change the phrase *make my English better* to *achieve this important goal.* (The reason for making this change is that *achieve* and *goal* sound better than the simple phrase *make my English better.*)
10. Begin one of your sentences with the phrase *for example.*

Improving My English

I think my English is all right, but I want to improve my skills. For instance, my reading skills are weak. I don't know much sophisticated vocabulary, and long sentences are difficult for me to understand. In particular, I have serious problems with idioms. In addition to reading, I know that I need to improve my speaking skills. Some sounds in English are difficult for me to pronounce. I have problems with the sounds of B and V. People can understand what I am trying to say, but I can sense confusion in their voices when I answer the telephone. They say that the first

---

(continued)

step in solving a problem is to recognize that you have a problem. I accept that I need to improve my English. I am ready to work hard to make my English better.

_____

_____

_____

_____

_____

_____

_____

_____

_____

_____

_____

_____

_____

_____

■ CHAPTER QUIZ

Exercise 24   **Part 1: Synthesis.** Circle the letter of the correct answer.

1. When I was in high school, my favorite class _____ .

   A. is American history   C. is history American

   B. was American history   D. was history American

2. Next year is our big vacation! My husband and I will be at _____ .

   A. the Hotel   C. four days in march

   B. the Hilton   D. four days in March

3. No one in my family is interested in _____, so we never talk about it.

    A. politic   C. political

    B. politics   D. politician

4. _____ in Minnesota are so cold, some retired people go to Florida from January to March.

    A. Because winters   C. Winters

    B. Because winter   D. Winter

5. Susan _____ to buy a hammer and some nails.

    A. went the hardware store yesterday   C. yesterday went to the hardware store

    B. yesterday to the hardware store went   D. went to the hardware store yesterday

6. I like your idea of buying an extra key for the front door. _____ with you about this.

    A. I am agreement   C. I agree

    B. Because I am agreement   D. Because I agree

Part 2: Error Correction. One of the four underlined words or phrases is not correct. Circle the letter of the error and correct it in the space provided.

7. You are going to go to San <u>Diego next</u> week, and <u>I go</u> to Houston. <u>Both of us are</u> going
                             A   **B**   **C**

    <u>to take a trip</u> somewhere. _____
      D

8. My friend <u>and I</u> bought an apartment <u>in Key West</u>, so I'm sure that <u>we will go</u> there
         A   **B**   **C**

    <u>on January</u>. _____
      D

9. I <u>really need</u> a vacation <u>from my job and</u> my classes. I need to <u>clear my</u> mind of all
      A   **B**   **C**

    <u>my problem</u>. _____
      D

10. The doctor gave <u>some chocolate</u> to the <u>two small</u> children in her office, and after
               A   **B**

    <u>that, were</u> really <u>quiet because they</u> were eating it. _____
      C   **D**

■ ORIGINAL WRITING

Exercise 25   On a separate sheet of paper, write an original paragraph (eight to twelve sentences) about a teacher that you know. We recommend that you double-space your writing to allow for teacher and peer editing and revisions.

In your writing, be sure to discuss why you chose this teacher. What good (or bad) qualities does the person possess? Give specific examples.

Focus on the correct use of the parts of speech, especially adjectives and verbs. Underline the verb(s) in each sentence.

Review of Verbs

In this chapter, you will review some of the most frequently used verb tenses in English.

2.1 Six Common Tenses in English

English has twelve verb tenses. In this chapter, you will review the six most frequently used verb tenses: simple present, present progressive, simple past, past progressive, present perfect, and simple future.

		Regular Verbs	Irregular Verbs
2.2	Simple present	I walk	I eat
2.3	Present progressive	I am walking	I am eating
2.4	Simple past	I walked	I ate
2.5	Past progressive	I was walking	I was eating
2.6	Present perfect	I have walked	I have eaten
2.7	Simple future	I will walk	I will eat
		I am going to walk	I am going to eat

2.2 Simple Present Tense

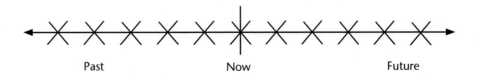

Past   Now   Future

Form for Regular Verbs

Base verb or verb + -s

Singular	Plural
I walk	we walk
you walk	you walk
he / she / it walks	they walk

Remember: The verb *to be* is irregular:

Singular	Plural
I am	we are
you are	you are
he / she / it is	they are

Remember:

1. If a verb ends in -o, add -es:

    I **go**, he **goes**;   I **do**, she **does**

2. If a verb ends in consonant + -y, change -y to -i and add -es:

    I **try**, he **tries**;   I **play**, she **plays**

3. The form of *have* with *he / she / it* is **has**, not *haves*.

Negative Form

To form the negative of most verbs in English, you add the helping verb *do / does* plus the negative marker *not*.

Remember: Helping verbs are needed for the negative form.

Singular	Plural
I **do not** walk	We **do not** walk
You **do not** walk	You **do not** walk
He / She / It **does not** walk	They **do not** walk

(The contractions *don't* for *do + not* and *doesn't* for *does + not* are not usually used in academic writing.)

When you use *does*, do not add -s to the base form of the verb.

    Incorrect: Mexico **does** not **produces** much rice.

    Correct: Mexico **does** not **produce** much rice.

Do not use *be* with the base form of the verb. Use *do / does* with the base form of the verb.

    Incorrect: April **is not have** 31 days.

    Correct: April **does not have** 31 days.

Question Form

To form a question, add the helping verb *do / does* to the beginning of the sentence:

Singular	Plural
Do I walk?	**Do** we walk?
Do you walk?	**Do** you walk?
Does he / she / it walk?	**Do** they walk?

When you use *does*, do not add *-s* to the base form of the verb.

Incorrect:	**Does** Mexico **produces** much rice?
Correct:	**Does** Mexico **produce** much rice?

Do not use *be* with the base form of the verb. Use *do / does* with the base form of the verb.

Incorrect:	~~Is~~ April **have** 31 days?
Correct:	**Does** April **have** 31 days?

Uses of the Simple Present

1. For facts that are not limited to a specific time; for general truths

   The President of the United States **lives** in the White House.

2. For a repeated, habitual, or usual action

   I **drive** to work at 7:00 a.m. every morning. I **do not take** the bus.

3. For information from a book, a poem, research, or other work (This is often called the literary present.)

   In the short story "The Necklace," Madame Loisel **dreams** of having a high-class lifestyle. She **does not feel** satisfied with her current life.

4. For the immediate future

   The movie **starts** in ten minutes.

Exercise 1   Fill in the correct forms of these verbs in the present tense. The first one has been done for you.

WRITE		
Affirmative	**Negative**	**Question**
I _write_	I _do not write_	_Do_ I _write_ ...?
You _____	You _____	_____ you _____ ...?
He _____	He _____	_____ he _____ ...?
She _____	She _____	_____ she _____ ...?

(continued)

WRITE

Affirmative	Negative	Question
It _____	It _____	_____ it _____ ...?
We _____	We _____	_____ we _____ ...?
You _____	You _____	_____ you _____ ...?
They _____	They _____	_____ they _____ ...?

TAKE

Affirmative	Negative	Question
I _____	I _____	_____ I _____ ...?
You _____	You _____	_____ you _____ ...?
He _____	He _____	_____ he _____ ...?
She _____	She _____	_____ she _____ ...?
It _____	It _____	_____ it _____ ...?
We _____	We _____	_____ we _____ ...?
You _____	You _____	_____ you _____ ...?
They _____	They _____	_____ they _____ ...?

HAVE

Affirmative	Negative	Question
I _____	I _____	_____ I _____ ...?
You _____	You _____	_____ you _____ ...?
He _____	He _____	_____ he _____ ...?
She _____	She _____	_____ she _____ ...?
It _____	It _____	_____ it _____ ...?
We _____	We _____	_____ we _____ ...?
You _____	You _____	_____ you _____ ...?
They _____	They _____	_____ they _____ ...?

DO		
Affirmative	**Negative**	**Question**
I _____	I _____	_____ I _____ ...?
You _____	You _____	_____ you _____ ...?
He _____	He _____	_____ he _____ ...?
She _____	She _____	_____ she _____ ...?
It _____	It _____	_____ it _____ ...?
We _____	We _____	_____ we _____ ...?
You _____	You _____	_____ you _____ ...?
They _____	They _____	_____ they _____ ...?

Exercise 2   Read the paragraph. Draw two lines under each simple present tense verb. There are twenty-five. The first one has been done for you.

A Typical College Weekday

Julian Wilson, a college student, <u>lives</u> with his sister, Joanne, in Austin, Texas.

His classes start at 8:00 a.m., so he wakes up very early. Julian takes a shower and

brushes his teeth, and then he puts on his school clothes. Julian has breakfast with

his sister, and they talk about their day. After breakfast, Joanne usually drives Julian

to the college because Julian does not know how to drive Joanne's car. He has classes

all morning and then meets his friends for lunch. Sometimes he and his friends eat

lunch in the cafeteria, but most of the time they go to a café off campus. Julian does

not have any classes after lunch, so he takes the bus home at 2:00 p.m. After that, he

does his homework and waits for his sister. Joanne is a great cook, and Julian usually

helps her in the kitchen. After dinner, he washes the dishes, and they watch TV for

an hour or so. Julian almost always checks his e-mail before bed. That is Julian's

schedule on weekdays. Of course his weekends are a little different.

Exercise 3   Write two sentences for each of the four uses of the simple present tense. The first one has been done for you. Use at least one negative form.

Use 1: Facts and General Truths

Sentence 1: _Brazilians speak Portuguese._

Sentence 2: _____

_____

Use 2: Repeated or Usual Action

Sentence 1: _____

_____

Sentence 2: _____

_____

Use 3: Literary Present

Sentence 1: _____

_____

Sentence 2: _____

_____

Use 4: Immediate Future

Sentence 1: _____

_____

Sentence 2: _____

_____

2.3   Present Progressive Tense

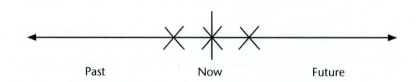

Past   Now   Future

Present Progressive Form

am / is / are + verb + *-ing*

Singular	Plural
I **am walking**	We **are walking**
You **are walking**	You **are walking**
He / She / It **is walking**	They **are walking**

Spelling the *-ing* form: If a verb ends in consonant + vowel + consonant (CVC), double the last consonant before adding *-ing:*

sit → si**tt**ing   clap → cla**pp**ing   begin → begi**nn**ing

If a verb has two syllables and ends in CVC, double the last consonant if the stress is on the second syllable. Compare these two-syllable verbs:

1 2   1 2
o pen → opening   be gin → beginning

We stress *open* on the first syllable, so we only add *-ing.*

We stress *begin* on the second syllable, so we double the *n* before adding *-ing* in *beginning.*

If a verb ends in consonant + *-e*, drop the *-e* and add *-ing:*

hope → ho**ping**   write → wri**ting**   produce → produ**cing**

Uses of the Present Progressive

1. For a temporary action that is happening at this moment and will have a definite end

For this type of temporary action, writers often use adverbs such as *now, right now, currently,* and *at this moment.*

The children **are playing** in the park *right now.* Their mother **is watching** them.

2. For a longer action that is happening at a particular time

For this type of longer action, writers often use adverbs such as *this month, today,* and *this year.*

Bobbie **is studying** for his final exams *this month.*

3. For an event in the near future (used with a time phrase to indicate future)

I **am leaving** for France *next week.*

When a verb does not express an action, it is usually not used in a progressive form. Common non-action verbs include *own, possess, have, be, prefer, like, love, want, need, desire, taste, smell, think,* and *feel.*

Incorrect: Most people ~~are preferring~~ the color silver for cars.

Correct: Most people **prefer** the color silver for cars.

Sometimes a verb can have both an action meaning and a non-action meaning.

Non-action: I **have** a dictionary and a magazine with me now.

Action: I **am having** a hard time in my chemistry class now.

Exercise 4 Fill in the correct forms of these verbs in present progressive tense. The first one has been done for you.

WRITE		
Affirmative	**Negative**	**Question**
I _am writing_	I _am not writing_	_Am_ I _writing_ ...?
You _____	You _____	_____ you _____ ...?
He _____	He _____	_____ he _____ ...?
She _____	She _____	_____ she _____ ...?
It _____	It _____	_____ it _____ ...?
We _____	We _____	_____ we _____ ...?
You _____	You _____	_____ you _____ ...?
They _____	They _____	_____ they _____ ...?

STOP (a verb showing other specified spelling pattern)		
Affirmative	**Negative**	**Question**
I _____	I _____	_____ I _____ ...?
You _____	You _____	_____ you _____ ...?
He _____	He _____	_____ he _____ ...?
She _____	She _____	_____ she _____ ...?
It _____	It _____	_____ it _____ ...?
We _____	We _____	_____ we _____ ...?
You _____	You _____	_____ you _____ ...?
They _____	They _____	_____ they _____ ...?

Exercise 5 Read the sentences about Canada and notice the underlined verbs. Write A, B, or AB to show which examples are correct. The first one has been done for you.

A	B

<u>AB</u> 1. Canada <u>exports</u> wheat.   Canada <u>is exporting</u> more wheat this year.

—— 2. Canada <u>has</u> ten provinces.   Canada <u>is having</u> ten provinces.

—— 3. All Canadian citizens <u>vote</u> secretly.   All Canadian citizens <u>are voting</u> today.

—— 4. All citizens <u>possess</u> special rights.   All citizens <u>are possessing</u> special rights.

—— 5. The Canadian flag <u>has</u> a   The Canadian flag <u>is having</u> a maple leaf.

maple leaf.

—— 6. Niagara Falls, Canada, <u>has</u>   The Canadian tourism industry <u>is having</u>

many tourists.   problems.

—— 7. Many tourists <u>think</u> that Niagara   Many tourists <u>are thinking</u> that Niagara

Falls is beautiful.   Falls is beautiful.

—— 8. We <u>think</u> about Canada a lot.   We <u>are thinking</u> about going to Canada

next week.

Exercise 6 Read the verbs in the box. In the spaces provided, write four sentences describing what you are doing *right now*. Use the present progressive form of the verbs in the box. The first one has been done for you.

sit	write	think (about)	copy	wear	smile	~~look at~~

1. Right now I am looking at this exercise. _____

2. _____

3. _____

4. _____

5. _____

Exercise 7   Read the sentences about Daunte's hobbies. Change the verbs from simple present to present progressive. Add the phrases in parentheses to your new sentences. In some cases, you need to substitute the new time phrase for the time phrase that is in the original sentence. The first one has been done for you.

1. My best friend Daunte works at a local bank. (this year) _My best friend Daunte is working_

at a local bank this year.

2. Daunte lives with his cousin. (this semester) _____

_____

3. They take a photography class together on Thursday nights. (next Thursday night) ____

_____

4. Daunte throws great parties at his house on weekends. (on Sunday) _____

_____

5. He often reads detective novels. (these days) _____

_____

6. He goes to a hockey game every Saturday night. (tonight) _____

_____

Exercise 8   Read the paragraph about our new pet. There are six mistakes in verb tense (present or present progressive). Find and correct the errors.

My Puppy

Our new puppy Lucky keeps the entire family very busy. Everyone in the family

is having his or her own responsibility with the puppy. My mother's job is to feed

Lucky. This is not an easy job because Lucky eats a lot. In fact, Mom feeds him right

now. My dad's job is to walk Lucky. Dad is taking Lucky for a walk around the block

---

(continued)

every evening. Lucky has short legs, so he does not walk very fast. We have to be

patient with Lucky because he is very curious and is stopping every ten seconds to

smell something. My job is to give Lucky a bath. This is probably the most difficult

job of all. Believe me, Lucky is not liking bath time. When he hears the water

running in the bathtub, he runs away. Actually, I fill the bathtub up with water right

this minute. Hey! Where is Lucky?

2.4   Simple Past Tense

Past   Now   Future

Form for Regular Verbs

verb + -ed

>   I **worked** at the restaurant.

Spelling the -ed form: If a verb ends in consonant + vowel + consonant, double the last consonant before adding -ed:

>   tip → tip**ped**   clap → clap**ped**   rob → rob**bed**

If a verb ends in consonant + -e, drop the -e and add -ed:

>   name → nam**ed**   create → creat**ed**   produce → produc**ed**

If a verb ends in consonant + -y, change the -y to -i and add -ed:

>   carry → carr**ied**   cry → cr**ied**   marry → marr**ied**

Form for Irregular Verbs

Irregular past tense verbs have different forms that you have to learn. There are about 140 irregular verbs in English, but only half of these are very common. Here is a list of some of the most commonly used irregular past tense forms.

base verb	past tense	base verb	past tense
be	was / were	have	had
do	did	know	knew
drink	drank	leave	left
drive	drove	make	made
eat	ate	meet	met
feel	felt	put	put
find	found	read	read
get	got	say	said
give	gave	speak	spoke
go	went	take	took

Negative Form

In the negative, add the helping verb *did* plus the negative marker *not*.

Singular	Plural
I **did not** walk	We **did not** walk
You **did not** walk	You **did not** walk
He / She / It **did not** walk	They **did not** walk

(The contraction *didn't* for *did* + *not* is not usually used in academic writing.)

With *did*, use the base form of the verb, not a past tense form.

> *Incorrect:*   Mexico (**did**) not **produce**(d) much oil before 1960.

> *Correct:*   Mexico **did** not **produce** much oil before 1960.

> *Incorrect:*   The runner from France (**did**) not (**took**) the first prize.

> *Correct:*   The runner from France **did** not **take** the first prize.

Do not confuse the verb *to be* with the helping verb *did*.

> *Incorrect*:   Germany ~~**was**~~ not **win** many silver medals.

> *Correct*:   Germany **did** not **win** many silver medals.

Question Form

To form a question, add the helping verb *did* to the beginning of the sentence:

Singular	Plural
Did I walk?	**Did** we walk?
Did you walk?	**Did** you walk?
Did he / she / it walk?	**Did** they walk?

With *did*, use the base form of the verb, not the past tense form.

Incorrect: Did Mexico **produced** fifty million tons of rice in 2000?

Correct: **Did** Mexico **produce** fifty million tons of rice in 2000?

Uses of the Simple Past

1. For an action or condition that was completed in the past

   People **discovered** gold in California in 1848.

2. For a series of finished actions

   Texas **became** a state in 1845, and California **joined** the United States in 1850.

Exercise 9 Fill in the correct forms of these verbs in simple past tense. The first one has been done for you.

WORK		
Affirmative	**Negative**	**Question**
I _worked_	I _did not work_	_Did_ I _work_ ...?
You _____	You _____	_____ you _____ ...?
He _____	He _____	_____ he _____ ...?
She _____	She _____	_____ she _____ ...?
It _____	It _____	_____ it _____ ...?
We _____	We _____	_____ we _____ ...?
You _____	You _____	_____ you _____ ...?
They _____	They _____	_____ they _____ ...?

REPLY (verb with different spelling pattern)		
Affirmative	**Negative**	**Question**
I _____	I _____	_____ I _____ ...?
You _____	You _____	_____ you _____ ...?
He _____	He _____	_____ he _____ ...?
She _____	She _____	_____ she _____ ...?
It _____	It _____	_____ it _____ ...?

(continued)

REPLY (verb with different spelling pattern)

Affirmative	Negative	Question
We _____	We _____	_____ we _____ ...?
You _____	You _____	_____ you _____ ...?
They _____	They _____	_____ they _____ ...?

HAVE (irregular verb)

Affirmative	Negative	Question
I _____	I _____	_____ I _____ ...?
You _____	You _____	_____ you _____ ...?
He _____	He _____	_____ he _____ ...?
She _____	She _____	_____ she _____ ...?
It _____	It _____	_____ it _____ ...?
We _____	We _____	_____ we _____ ...?
You _____	You _____	_____ you _____ ...?
They _____	They _____	_____ they _____ ...?

DO (irregular verb)

Affirmative	Negative	Question
I _____	I _____	_____ I _____ ...?
You _____	You _____	_____ you _____ ...?
He _____	He _____	_____ he _____ ...?
She _____	She _____	_____ she _____ ...?
It _____	It _____	_____ it _____ ...?
We _____	We _____	_____ we _____ ...?
You _____	You _____	_____ you _____ ...?
They _____	They _____	_____ they _____ ...?

Exercise 10 The following paragraph is similar to the paragraph in Exercise 2, page 27. However, this paragraph is in the past tense. Read the paragraph and fill in the missing past tense verbs (both regular and irregular). If you need help choosing a verb, refer to the original paragraph on page 27. The first one has been done for you.

Memories of College Life

Julian Wilson, who was a college student, _____lived_____ with his
1

sister, Joanne, in Austin, Texas, for four years. His classes _____
2

at 8:00 a.m., so he woke up very early. Julian _____ a shower
3

and _____ his teeth, and then he _____ on
4   5

his school clothes. Julian _____ breakfast with his sister, and
6

they _____ about their day. After breakfast, Joanne usually
7

_____ Julian to the college in her car. He _____
8   9

classes all morning. After that, he _____ his friends for lunch.
10

Sometimes they _____ lunch in the cafeteria, but most of the
11

time they _____ to a café off campus. At 4:00 p.m., Julian
12

_____ to the library, and he _____ for his sister
13   14

to pick him up. Joanne is a great cook, and Julian usually _____
15

her in the kitchen. After dinner, he _____ the dishes, and they
16

_____ TV for an hour or so. Both Julian and Joanne normally
17

_____ to sleep around 11:00 p.m. That _____
18   19

Julian's systematic schedule during college.

Exercise 11   Read the sentences about a vacation in New Mexico. Write the correct past tense form of the verbs in parentheses. The first one has been done for you.

1. I (take) _____took_____ my favorite vacation in the summer of 2003.

2. I (go) _____ with my family to Carlsbad Caverns in Carlsbad,

   New Mexico.

3. The vacation (last) _____ for three weeks. Imagine! I (do, neg)

   _____ any work for 21 days!

4. We (drive) _____ from Florida to New Mexico and (stay)

   _____ in hotels for the entire trip.

5. My parents (be) _____ in one room, and my brothers and I (sleep)

   _____ in another room.

6. When we (get) _____ to the Caverns, we (see)

   _____ many incredible rock formations.

7. I (feel) _____ so sad when it (be) _____ time to

   go home.

8. I (want, neg) _____ to leave.

9. It (be) _____ incredible!

10. We (have) _____ a great time.

Exercise 12   Write five sentences about your favorite vacation. Use the simple past tense.

1. _____

2. _____

3. _____

4. _____

5. _____

2.5   Past Progressive Tense

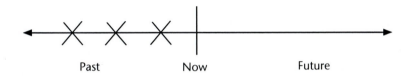

Past   Now   Future

Form for Regular Verbs

was / were + verb + *-ing*

> I **was working.**

Negative Form

Use *not* after *was* or *were*. The contractions *wasn't* for *was not* and *weren't* for *were not* are not common in academic writing.

> Colombia played a friendly soccer match against France last week. After ten minutes of play, it was clear that France **was not playing** well.

> When I checked the score after halftime, the Colombian fans **were not cheering** anymore. The French scored two goals in the first half of the game.

Question Form

To make a question, invert the subject and the form of *be*.

> [It was raining] **Was** it **raining** very hard when Flight 822 made an emergency landing?

> [Other planes were flying] **Were** any other planes **flying** near Flight 822 at that time?

Uses of the Past Progressive

1. For an action in the past that was interrupted

    We **were working** in the backyard when the dark clouds appeared.

2. For an action that was happening at a specific time

    At 6:00 p.m. last night, we **were working** in the backyard.

3. For background or atmosphere information when you are describing a scene or telling a story

    When I walked into the classroom, I immediately became worried. The professor **was writing** tiny lecture notes on the blackboard, some students **were napping** in their chairs, and the class syllabus, which was at least 10 pages long, **was lying** on everyone's desk.

Exercise 13 Fill in the correct forms of these verbs in past progressive tense. The first one has been done for you.

TAKE		
Affirmative	**Negative**	**Question**
I _was taking_	I _was not taking_	_Was_ I _taking_ ...?
You _____	You _____	_____ you _____ ...?
He _____	He _____	_____ he _____ ...?
She _____	She _____	_____ she _____ ...?
It _____	It _____	_____ it _____ ...?
We _____	We _____	_____ we _____ ...?
You _____	You _____	_____ you _____ ...?
They _____	They _____	_____ they _____ ...?

DO		
Affirmative	**Negative**	**Question**
I _____	I _____	_____ I _____ ...?
You _____	You _____	_____ you _____ ...?
He _____	He _____	_____ he _____ ...?
She _____	She _____	_____ she _____ ...?

(continued)

DO		
Affirmative	**Negative**	**Question**
It _____	It _____	_____ it _____ ...?
We _____	We _____	_____ we _____ ...?
You _____	You _____	_____ you _____ ...?
They _____	They _____	_____ they _____ ...?

Exercise 14   Read the following scenarios. Then answer the questions using the past progressive tense. The first one has been done for you.

1. I tried to find you last night. What were you doing? _I was writing an essay in the_

   computer lab.

2. I waited for you at the library for three hours last night. What were you doing? _____

   _____

3. I tried to call your cell phone at least three times. Was your cell phone working? _____

   _____

4. Then I called your home phone, but it was busy. Who were you talking to? _____

   _____

5. After that I drove to your house and saw your car pulling out of the driveway. Where were you going? _____

   _____

6. I drove by your house again later that night and saw there was a light on inside the house. Were you watching TV? What were you watching? _____

   _____

7. I got out of the car and knocked on your door, but you didn't answer. Were you sleeping? _____

   _____

2.6 Present Perfect Tense

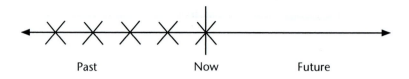

Past   Now   Future

Form for Regular Verbs

have / has + past participle (See Notes on the Past Participle section that follows.)

I **have worked.**

Negative Form

The negative of *have* in present perfect is *have not / has not*. The contractions *haven't* for *have not* and *hasn't* for *has not* are not common in academic writing.

Singular	Plural
I **have not** walked	We **have not** walked
You **have not** walked	You **have not** walked
He / She / It **has not** walked	They **have not** walked

Sentences containing the verb *have* as the main verb may look odd in the present perfect. However, this construction is correct.

I **have had** many great cups of espresso since I arrived here in Italy.

Uses of the Present Perfect

1. For an action that started in the past and continues in the present (This particular use often includes the phrases "*since* + a specific time" or "*for* + length of time")

   California **has been** a state *since* 1850.

   California **has been** a state *for* more than 150 years.

2. For an action that has just been completed (often using *just*)

   We **have** *just* **finished** working.

3. For a past action that still has an effect on the present

   The company **lost** revenue, so management **has fired** many employees.

4. For an action that happened several times (no specific past time) and may happen again (indefinite past)

   We **have eaten** at that restaurant five times.

5. For an action that happened in the past, but the time or frequency of the action is not important (often used with *ever* or *never*) (indefinite past)

   Julia **has** *never* **visited** Las Vegas, but she would like to.

   Have you *ever* **driven** an Italian sports car?

Notes on the Past Participle

Regular Verbs: The past participle of regular verbs is formed exactly like the simple past tense of regular verbs: verb + -*ed*

Base		Past		Past Participle
work	→	work**ed**	→	work**ed**
arrive	→	arriv**ed**	→	arriv**ed**
study	→	stud**ied**	→	stud**ied**

Irregular Verbs: Common ways of forming the past participle of irregular verbs are -*en* and -*ne*. Some irregular verbs have vowel changes (*i* → *a* → *u*). Other verbs keep the base form for the past and the past participle.

Base		Past		Past Participle
choose	→	chose	→	cho**sen**
go	→	went	→	go**ne**
sing	→	sang	→	s**u**ng
fly	→	flew	→	fl**own**
put	→	**put**	→	**put**
tell	→	**told**	→	**told**

Review the forms of these twenty irregular verbs.

Base Verb	Past Tense	Past Participle	Base Verb	Past Tense	Past Participle
be	was / were	**been**	know	knew	**known**
become	became	**become**	leave	left	**left**
do	did	**done**	make	made	**made**
drive	drove	**driven**	put	put	**put**
feel	felt	**felt**	read	read	**read**
find	found	**found**	say	said	**said**
get	got	**gotten**	see	saw	**seen**
give	gave	**given**	speak	spoke	**spoken**
go	went	**gone**	take	took	**taken**
have	had	**had**	write	wrote	**written**

Exercise 15   Read the sentences about a trip. Underline the present perfect verbs. The first one has been done for you.

1. My best friend from the university <u>has invited</u> me to visit her during spring break.

2. She has traveled all over the world.

3. I have never been outside my own country.

4. In fact, I have never even flown on an airplane before (and I am afraid!).

5. My travel agent has already purchased the tickets for me.

6. I have not told my friend this yet.

7. I have considered just staying home for this vacation.

8. Have you ever had this problem?

Exercise 16 Read this paragraph about how to cook one kind of food. There are ten verb tense errors (simple present, present progressive, present perfect, and simple past). Find and correct the errors. The numbers on the left tell you how many errors are in the line.

A Quick Recipe

Cooking a meal for your friends is a great way to show them how much you care.

1   For anyone who do not, or cannot cook, here is a dish that is simple and tasty and

1   inexpensive to make. I have name this dish "Quick Quesadillas." Believe me, if you

1   can pronounce this word, then you can make this dish. First, you are need to buy

1   a package of tortillas, which is a type of thin round bread that was made of corn or

flour. Next, you will need some cheese. Put a pan on the stove and turn the fire up to

medium heat. Spray the pan with light vegetable oil and let the pan heat up. Please

(continued)

1	do not use butter. I try that one time. It was a disaster. While the pan is getting hot,
	grate the cheese. Take a tomato and chop it into little cubes and save it for the end. If
2	you wanting your friends to think that you were a professional chef, add a few leaves
1	of cilantro to the chopped tomato. Once the pan is being hot, lay one tortilla in
	the pan and sprinkle the cheese on top. Cover the cheese with a second tortilla and
	push the two tortillas together with a spatula. Wait for the cheese to melt. When this
1	happen, turn the tortillas over and let the other side cook for another minute. Then
1	you are taking the quesadilla out of the pan and cut it into four slices like a little
	pizza. Add the chopped tomatoes and cilantro on top and serve. Your friends will
	love it and love you!

2.7 Simple Future Tense

Past   Now   Future

Two Forms for the Future

The future tense takes two general forms:

be going to + verb

    The exam **is going to begin** at noon.

and *will* + verb

    The exam **will begin** at noon.

Uses of Future Tense

1. For a future plan

   I **am going to go** to the beach next weekend.

   I **will go** to the beach next weekend.

   The race **is going to be** one of the most exciting of the year!

   The race **will be** one of the most exciting of the year!

2. For a prediction

   In the next decade, electronics **are going to decrease** in price.

   In the next decade, electronics **will decrease** in price.

   Small pets **are going to be** much more popular as people move into big cities.

   Small pets **will be** much more popular as people move into big cities.

Exercise 17   Fill in the correct forms of these verbs in future tense. The first one has been done for you.

TAKE (use *will*)		
Affirmative	**Negative**	**Question**
I _will take_	I _will not take_	_Will_ I take ...?
You _____	You _____	_____ you _____ ...?
He _____	He _____	_____ he _____ ...?
She _____	She _____	_____ she _____ ...?
It _____	It _____	_____ it _____ ...?
We _____	We _____	_____ we _____ ...?
You _____	You _____	_____ you _____ ...?
They _____	They _____	_____ they _____ ...?

HAVE (use *be going to*)		
Affirmative	**Negative**	**Question**
I _am going to have_	I _____	_____ I _____ ...?
You _____	You _____	_____ you _____ ...?
He _____	He _____	_____ he _____ ...?

(continued)

HAVE (use *be going to*)		
Affirmative	**Negative**	**Question**
She _____	She _____	_____ she _____ ...?
It _____	It _____	_____ it _____ ...?
We _____	We _____	_____ we _____ ...?
You _____	You _____	_____ you _____ ...?
They _____	They _____	_____ they _____ ...?

Exercise 18 Read the sentences about a lawyer and notice the underlined verbs. Rewrite each sentence using the future form *be going to* + verb. Be sure to notice the phrases that have been added to your new sentences. The first one has been done for you.

1. I <u>work</u> in a busy law firm.

   After college, I am going to work in a busy law firm.

2. My brother <u>has not finished</u> college yet.

   _____ for two more years.

3. I <u>have worked</u> night and day as a lawyer.

   My brother tells me that _____

4. I <u>enjoyed</u> putting dangerous criminals in prison.

   As a prosecutor, _____

5. I <u>make</u> a lot of money.

   Even better, _____

6. I <u>do not waste</u> my money on silly material things that I do not need.

   When I am rich, _____

7. I <u>am quitting</u> my job, and I <u>am traveling</u> all over the world.

   In a few years, _____

8. I <u>bought</u> a little house on the beach and retire.

   When I return from my round-the-world vacation, _____

   _____

Exercise 19 Read this paragraph about a hobby. Circle the correct form of the verbs in parentheses. You will have a choice of using the simple present, present progressive, simple past, present perfect, and future tense. The first one has been done for you.

Reading for Pleasure

It seems that people (were not reading / (are not reading)) as many books
1

nowadays as they used to. Some people claim that this (was happening / is happening)
2

because books take too much time to read. It is certainly true that most people simply

(do not have / did not have) much free time anymore. Others say that most of the good
3

books have been turned into movies anyway. These people (believe / are believing) that
4

it is easier to just watch the movie. In addition, there are many new forms of

high-tech entertainment that (were replacing / have replaced) books as the preferred
5

leisure activity. Cinema, TV, music videos, video games and the Internet are, for young

people of today, what books (are / were) for past generations.
6

■ GUIDED WRITING

Exercise 20 Read the paragraph below. Rewrite it by making the five changes listed. Careful! You may have to make other changes.

1. Change *next year* to *last year.*

2. Change all of the future verb tenses to past tense.

3. Insert the adverb of time phrase *for a day or two* after the word *there.*

4. Combine the information in sentences 7 and 8.

5. Replace the adjective *incredible* with another adjective.

6. Change *every item of food* to *all the varieties of food.*

Alaskan Vacation

Next year I am going to take a cruise to Alaska. It is going to be a magnificent trip. I will save money from my part-time job as a cashier at the college bookstore. First, I will fly to Anchorage from Chicago. I am going to stay there to see the local sights. After that, I will head to the port to board the ship. This particular cruise liner is one of the largest in the world. It has twelve floors and space for over 3,000 guests. I will pay extra to get a cabin with a balcony because the views of the glaciers are supposed to be incredible! Finally, I am going to go on a strict diet at least one month before the cruise. If nothing else, I want to taste every item of food that I will find on the ship.

_____

_____

_____

_____

_____

_____

_____

_____

_____

_____

_____

_____

_____

_____

Exercise 21 **Part 1: Synthesis.** Circle the letter of the correct answer.

1. When Sammy started his studies at Rice University, he _____ biology as his college

   major.

   A. choose   C. chose

   B. has chosen   D. chooses

2. Excuse me. I'm looking for Gate 73. _____ you know where Gate 73 is?

   A. Are   C. Did

   B. Do   D. Were

3. My professor _____ to school by bike. I see her pedaling down the street

   every day.

   A. come   C. coming

   B. is come   D. comes

4. Winters in Washington, D.C., are not so cold. In fact, it _____ snow very often.

   A. does not   C. is not

   B. do not   D. not

5. When I _____ a child, pizza _____ my favorite food.

   A. was / were   C. were / is

   B. was / was   D. were / was

6. I _____ to Germany next year.

   A. will going   C. will

   B. am going   D. go

Part 2: Error Correction. One of the four underlined words or phrases is not correct.
Circle the letter of the error and correct it in the space provided.

7. I <u>love going</u> to the beach. It <u>make me</u> so happy to hear <u>the ocean</u> and play in <u>the sand</u>.
        A   **B**   **C**   **D**

   _____

8. Lisa <u>was only seven years</u> old when she <u>moved to</u> Canada, but she already <u>speak</u>
           A   **B**   **C**
   French fluently because her mother <u>was born</u> in Quebec.
                             D

   _____

9. Larry <u>not come</u> to class yesterday because he <u>had a cold</u>. I <u>think</u> he <u>is feeling</u>
      A   **B**   **C**   **D**

    better today. _____

10. We <u>ate</u> and <u>danced</u> too much at my sister's wedding, but it <u>was</u> a great celebration.
      A   **B**   **C**

    We <u>didn't left</u> until midnight! _____
         D

■ ORIGINAL WRITING

Exercise 22   On a separate sheet of paper, write an original paragraph (five to eight sentences) about your favorite movie.

Discuss when you saw the movie (focus on past tense verbs). Briefly describe the movie's plot, using the present and present progressive tenses. Be sure to explain *why* this movie is special to you. Underline the verb(s) in each sentence.

3 Nouns and Articles

You learned in Chapter 1 that the verb is the most important word in a sentence (see page 1). The second most important word in a sentence is a **noun**. Along with nouns, you need to learn the choice and placement of **articles**.

3.1 Noun Basics

A **noun** is the name of a person, place, thing, idea, or feeling.

person:	woman	children	Dr. Smith	Mrs. Williams
place:	downtown	the beach	Boston	Dallas
thing:	a cup	a drink	Pepsi-Cola	Delta Airlines
idea / feeling:	honesty	friendship	happiness	anger

Exercise 1   Read the sentences about Colombia. Fill in the blanks with the correct noun from the box. The first one has been done for you.

Cali	capital	city	country	~~country~~
Colombians	language	people	Spanish	Spanish

1. Colombia is a ____country____ in South America.

2. The _____ is Bogota.

3. People from Colombia are called _____ .

4. The official _____ is _____ .

5. In fact, almost 100 percent of the _____ speak

   _____ .

6. _____ is the second largest _____ in

   this _____ .

Colombia

SOUTH
AMERICA

3.2   Count Nouns

Nouns that name things you can count are called **count nouns.** Count nouns can be singular or plural.

singular:	a pencil	a quiz	my baby	one child
plural:	some pencils	ten quizzes	our babies	many children

3.2.1   *Singular Count Nouns*

All singular count nouns **must** have an article (*a, an, the*) or some other determiner before them. (See Sections 3.3 and 3.5 for more about articles.)

determiner	without a descriptive adjective	with a descriptive adjective
articles	a cat	a black cat
possessive	my class	my worst class
demonstrative	that book	that interesting book
number	one reason	one specific reason
quantifier	each problem	each serious problem

(Note: <u>Determiner</u> is a large category that includes (1) articles: *a, an, the;* (2) possessive adjectives: *my, your, his, her, its, our, their;* (3) demonstratives: *this, that, these, those;* (4) numbers: *one, two, three;* (5) quantifiers: *each, many, several.*)

Do not use a singular count noun without an article or other determiner:

Incorrect:	~~black cat~~	~~worst class~~	~~interesting book~~	~~reason~~
Correct:	a black cat	my worst class	an interesting book	the reason

In some idiomatic expressions, no article is used:

have dinner	in school	on vacation	at home	at work	by phone

Exercise 2   Read the paragraphs about English grammar. Underline the singular count nouns and circle their determiners. Paragraph 1 has thirteen singular count nouns, paragraph 2 has thirteen, and paragraph 3 has four. The first sentence has been done for you. (Hint: *part of speech* is actually a compound noun here; speech is not a separate noun here.)

Parts of Speech

What is (a) <u>part</u> of speech? English has eight parts of speech. A noun is the

name of a person, a place, a thing, an idea, or a feeling. Nouns might be the most

common part of speech. A verb is a word that expresses an action. Verbs are very

important to every sentence.

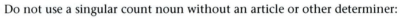

(continued)

In addition to nouns and verbs, there are pronouns, adjectives, and adverbs.

A pronoun is a word that can replace a noun. Some examples of pronouns are the words *she* and *they*. An adjective describes a noun or a pronoun. Adverbs sometimes end in the letters *-ly*. A good example of an adjective and an adverb is in the phrase *extremely hungry*. In this example, *extremely* is an adverb and *hungry* is an adjective.

The last three parts of speech in this list of eight forms are prepositions, conjunctions, and interjections. Prepositions are small words such as *in, at*, and *on*. Conjunctions include *and, or, but*, and *so*. Interjections are a group of words that express a strong feeling or an emotion. Words such as *oh!* qualify as interjections.

3.2.2   *Plural Count Nouns*

To make a noun **plural**, you usually add *-s*.

> book → books   eraser → erasers   subject → subject**s**

If a noun ends in *-s, -ss, -x, -ch, -sh* or *–z*, we add *-es* to make the plural form.*

> bu<u>s</u> → bus**es**   ki<u>ss</u> → kiss**es**   toolbo<u>x</u> → toolbox**es**
>
> swit<u>ch</u> → switch**es**   bu<u>sh</u> → bush**es**   qui<u>z</u> → quizz**es**

Exercise 3   Write the plural form of each noun to the right of its singular form. The first one has been done for you.

singular	plural
1. computer	computers
2. watch	_____
3. word	_____
4. action	_____
5. dress	_____
6. lunch	_____

---

*Exception: when the final *-ch* sounds like /k/, just add *-s*.
> stomach → stomach<u>s</u>

7. monarch   _____

8. arch   _____

9. loss   _____

10. plate   _____

11. dish   _____

12. bowl   _____

13. pan   _____

14. fox   _____

Exercise 4   A student wrote these sentences about her science class. However, she forgot to use plural nouns. Circle the eight mistakes and write the correct plural above each mistake. Hint: Some sentences have more than one mistake, and some sentences are correct. The first one has been done for you.

days

1. My science class meets three (day) every week.

2. My science class lasts for two hour.

3. It begins at 8:00 a.m. and finishes at 10:00 a.m.

4. The classroom is very large.

5. The classroom has thirty desk, but there are only twenty-three student in our class.

6. This means that there are seven place where no one sits.

7. Dr. Sanders, who is our science professor, is very good, but she is strict.

8. For example, we have a quiz every Friday.

9. On last week's quiz, we had many difficult question, but Dr. Sanders gave us only a

   short time to complete them.

10. On many of the quiz, my score are good, but my score on last week's quiz was not so good.

3.2.3　　*Other Spelling Changes in Noun Plurals*

Some nouns change their spelling to form the plural.

1. Nouns that end in -*y*

When the letter before -*y* is a vowel (*a, e, i, o, u*), just add -*s* to form the plural.

> boy → boy**s**　　day → day**s**　　bay → bay**s**

When the letter before -*y* is a consonant, change -*y* to -*i* and add -*es*.

> baby → bab**ies**　　city → cit**ies**　　lady → lad**ies**

2. Nouns that end in -*f* or -*fe*

The ending -*f* or -*fe* changes to -*ves* to form the plural.

> shelf → shel**ves**　　knife → kni**ves**　　leaf → lea**ves**

3. Nouns that have the same form for singular and plural

> 1 sheep → 2 sheep　　1 deer → 2 deer　　　1 fish → 3 fish

> 1 series → 2 series　　1 species → 10 species

4. Nouns with consonant + -*o* ending

Add -*es* to form the plural.

> hero → hero**es**　　potato → potato**es**

> echo → echo**es**　　mosquito → mosquito**es**

5. Nouns that have irregular spellings for the plural form

> mouse → **mice**　　child → **children**　　person → **people**

> man → **men**　　woman → **women**

> goose → **geese**　　foot → **feet**　　tooth → **teeth**

Exercise 5　　Write the plural form of these nouns that end in -*y*. The first one has been done for you.

singular	plural
1. a wild monkey	four wild ___monkeys___
2. one try	three _____
3. a new toy	two new _____
4. a fly	some _____
5. a baby	two _____
6. that lady	those _____
7. a bay	several _____
8. a bully	a few _____
9. this turkey	these _____

10. an interesting biography   two interesting _____

11. a long reply   many long _____

12. a very difficult day   very difficult _____

Exercise 6   Write the plural form of the noun in each phrase. The first one has been done for you.

singular	plural
1. a long life	long ___*lives*___
2. a wolf	some _____
3. herself	them _____
4. yourself	your _____
5. one leaf	many _____
6. one wife	four _____
7. a new scarf	new _____
8. a loaf of bread	five _____ of bread
9. a calf	nine _____
10. one half	three _____
11. one fish	five _____
12. a species of bird	one hundred _____ of birds
13. a mosquito	too many _____
14. a baked potato	six baked _____

Exercise 7   Write the singular or plural form of each noun. The first one has been done for you.

singular	plural
1. a mouse	four ___*mice*___
2. a _____	five men
3. a smart _____	smart children
4. one tooth	thirty-two _____
5. a _____	two geese
6. a tall woman	tall _____

7. a broken foot   two broken _____

8. one person   many _____

3.3   Articles *a* and *an*

The **articles *a*** and ***an*** are used only before singular count nouns. Specifically, use *a* and *an* with singular count nouns that are not specific and are being mentioned for the first time.

A dictionary has thousands of words and their meanings.

A cat has whiskers.

An umbrella is necessary when it rains hard.

Use *a* before a word (noun, or adjective + noun) that begins with a consonant sound.

a *dictionary*   **a *big dictionary***

Use *an* before a word (noun, or adjective + noun) that begins with a vowel sound.

an *orange*   **an *expensive orange***

Remember that words beginning with the letters *h* or *u* can be tricky. Some of these words use *a* and some use *an*—depending on the beginning sound of the word.

a *house*   **an *hour***

House begins with the consonant sound / h /, but *hour* begins with a vowel sound. (The letter *h* is silent in the word *hour*.)

a *university*   **an *uncle***

University begins with the consonant sound / y /, but *uncle* begins with a vowel sound.

Exercise 8   Fill in the blanks with *a* or *an*. Pay attention to the sound of the next word. The first one has been done for you.

1. __*an*__ examination

2. _____ history examination

3. _____ hard examination

4. _____ dictionary

5. _____ very useful dictionary

6. _____ useful dictionary

7. _____ student

8. _____ angry student

9. _____ heavy table

10. _____ extremely heavy table

11. _____ old man

12. _____ globe

13. _____ antique globe

14. _____ university

15. _____ university student

16. _____ honor student

17. _____ instructor

18. _____ horrible teacher

19. _____ professor

20. _____ whiteboard

Exercise 9 Read these sentences about superstitions. Complete each one with *a* or *an*. The first one has been done for you.

1. _____A_____ superstition is _____a_____ belief that is based on fear.

2. If you walk under _____ ladder, you will have bad luck.

3. If _____ black cat crosses your path, beware.

4. _____ apple _____ day keeps the doctor away.

5. _____ broken mirror will bring seven years of bad luck.

6. If you open _____ umbrella in the house, you will have bad luck.

7. _____ hat on _____ bed will bring bad luck.

8. To ward off bad luck, throw _____ pinch of salt over your shoulder.

9. If you see _____ owl in the daytime, it's bad luck.

10. It is good luck to find _____ four-leaf clover.

3.4	**Noncount Nouns**

Nouns that cannot be counted are called **noncount nouns**. Noncount nouns can refer to:

ideas	intelligence	peace	honesty	importance
sports	tennis	football	running	swimming
terms in nature	snow	thunder	electricity	water
subjects	mathematics	engineering	English	history
collective words	luggage	furniture	advice	homework

Do not use *a* or *an* with a noncount noun. Do not make a noncount noun plural.

| *Incorrect:* | ~~a homework~~ | ~~many furnitures~~ | ~~a mail~~ | ~~some equipments~~ |
| *Correct:* | homework | furniture | mail | equipment |

When the subject of a sentence is a noncount noun, remember to use the third person singular verb form. This is the same verb form that goes with the subject *it*.

Incorrect: Bread ~~are~~ my favorite snack.

Correct: Bread **is** my favorite snack.

Hint: It _____ my favorite snack. *Think:* Would you use *is* or *are* with *it*? Say *It is.* Do not say *It are.*

Exercise 10   Write C after count nouns and N after noncount nouns. The first two have been done for you. Be prepared to discuss your answers.

1. planet ___C___   11. grammar _____

2. sunshine ___N___   12. sentence _____

3. blood _____   13. pickle _____

4. bone _____   14. salt _____

5. truck _____   15. scenery _____

6. traffic _____   16. skyline _____

7. music _____   17. gem _____

8. song _____   18. jewelry _____

9. breath _____   19. good time _____

10. air _____   20. joke _____

Exercise 11   Read the sentences about engineering. Underline each noun. Write C above count nouns and N above noncount nouns. The number in parentheses at the end of each sentence indicates the number of nouns in that sentence. The first one has been done for you.

      N   C   C

1. <u>Engineering</u> is an important <u>subject</u> at most <u>universities</u>. (3)

2. A mechanical engineer may design machinery that we use in our homes and offices. (4)

3. A civil engineer may develop a road pattern for traffic that helps to save lives. (4)

4. Oxygen is an important element that is studied by a chemical engineer. (3)

5. An aeronautical engineer studies aircraft navigation. (2)

6. These different kinds of engineering are all important to modern society. (3)

3.5 The Article *the*

The **article *the*** is used before nouns at different times.

1. Use *the* when you are talking about something specific.

general:	Everyone has **an** identification card.
specific:	**The** identification card that you have is light blue.

2. Use *the* with the superlative form of an adjective, which means with the word *most* or *least* or with the ending *-est*.

comparative:	In a jewelry store, gold is more expensive than silver.
superlative:	In a jewelry store, diamonds are **the** most expensive material.
comparative:	In our class, Jan is tall, but Mark is taller.
superlative:	In our class, Ricky is **the** tallest student.

3. Use *the* for the second and all other references to a noun.

first reference:	We watched **a** video in our history class yesterday.
second reference:	**The** video lasted for about twenty minutes.

4. When you want to talk about a category or group in general, use no article.

general:	Tigers are fierce animals.
specific:	**The** tigers in our local zoo are fierce.

5. Use *the* when the speaker and the listener are talking about the same specific item.

general:	Every kitchen has **a** refrigerator.
specific:	William, don't forget to close **the** refrigerator!

6. Use *the* for the parts of something. (Exception: Do not use *the* for body parts.)

general:	In a kitchen, there is a refrigerator, a stove, and a clock.
parts:	I went to Mary's new house last night. Her kitchen is beautiful.
	The refrigerator is silver, **the** stove is black, and **the** clock above **the** door has extremely big numbers on it.

❗ Do not use *the* before abstract nouns such as feelings or ideas.

Incorrect:	~~The~~ honesty is important.
Correct:	Honesty is important.

❗ Do not use *the* with a word when you want to express a general meaning of the word.

Incorrect:	My favorite color is ~~the~~ blue.
Correct:	My favorite color is blue.
Incorrect:	I like ~~the~~ ice cream. I love ~~the~~ chocolate, but I don't like ~~the~~ vanilla.
Correct:	I like ice cream. I love chocolate, but I don't like vanilla.

Exercise 12 Read this short essay about classes. Fill in the blanks with *a, an, the,* or — (no article). The first one has been done for you.

My Classes

I have __—__ three classes on __—__ Monday. My math class is at __—__
    1   **2**   **3**

8:00 a.m. I like __—__ math. I think that __—__ math is very important for my
          4   **5**

future. In my math class, we learn about __—__ algebra and __—__ geometry.
                                 6   **7**

To me, __—__ algebra is more difficult than __—__ geometry. **The** hardest
      8   **9**   **(10)**

thing in __—__ algebra is when we have to solve problems with __—__ letters
       11   **12**

such as __—__ *x* and __—__ *y*. I like **the** book that we use in our math class
       13   **14**   **15**

because it has **a** key in **the** back of **the** book.
            16   **17**   **18**

In our history class yesterday, we had **an** important examination. **The**
                              19   **20**

test had thirty questions. The test had **a** long essay question at **the** end.
                                  21   **22**

To me, this question was **the** easiest question on **the** entire test.
                           23   **24**

One of **the** most interesting classes that I have is __—__ composition.
          25   **26** *writing*

This is **the** last class that I have on __—__ Thursday. __—__ last week we
     27   **28**   **29**

had to write **a** composition about **the** value of __—__ education.
             30   **31**   **32**

To help us with our paper, **the** instructor asked us to give some ideas. As we
                           33
                                   of the class

gave our ideas, he wrote them on **the** board. **The** purpose of this activity
                                  34   **35**

was to help us develop our thoughts. My paper got **a** good score.
                                       36

(continued)

_____ comments that _____ teacher wrote were very helpful. _____ topic
   37   38   39

of our next composition is up to us. I think that I am going to write about _____
       40

discrimination or _____ poverty. I know that these topics are serious, but I think
    41

that _____ writing about _____ serious topic such as _____ discrimination
    42   43   44

will force me to improve and then I can write _____ really good essay on _____
       45   46

final exam.

Exercise 13   Fill in the blanks with *a, an, the,* or — (no article). The first one has been done for you.

Staying Healthy

_____A_____ friend of mine and I were talking _____ yesterday about _____
   1   2   3

health. She asked me what I do to stay healthy. I told her that I do _____ exercises
       4

about _____ three or four times each week. In _____ morning, I get up early,
   5   6

drink _____ cup of _____ coffee, and then go running. I run _____ two miles
   7   8   9

because I think that _____ running is _____ best exercise that _____ person
      10   11   12

can do. During _____ time that I am running, I also have _____ chance to
    13   14

think about _____ things. Sometimes I think about _____ work, but mostly
    15   16

I think about _____ important things like my _____ family. In addition
    17   18

to _____ exercise, _____ food is also important. I believe that eating _____
   19   20   21

(continued)

fruit and _____ vegetables is essential to _____ good health. Yes, I eat _____
22   23   24

meat, but I do not eat a lot of it. As you can see, my plan for staying healthy

depends on _____ good exercise and _____ food. It is important for _____
25   26   27

people to select _____ plan that is easy so that they can follow it.
28

Review of Articles with Nouns

Count nouns				Noncount nouns	
General		Specific		General	Specific
Singular	*Plural*	*Singular*	*Plural*		
a cat	cats	the cat	the cats	—bread	the bread*
an apple	apples	the apple	the apples	—love	—love*

Exercise 14   Write a sentence with each of these examples to illustrate the differences between *a, an, the,* and no article. Discuss your sentences with your classmates. The first one has been done for you.

1. a book   *I found a great book on archeology in the library.*

2. books _____

   _____

3. the book _____

   _____

4. the books _____

   _____

5. vocabulary _____

   _____

_____

*We use *the* with specific cases of noncount nouns, but we almost never use *the* with abstract nouns such as feelings or ideas.

Incorrect:	All humans need ~~the~~ love.
Correct:	All humans need love.
Correct:	The strong love that you feel for your child is natural for parents.

6. the vocabulary _____

_____

7. education _____

_____

3.7 Quantifiers with Count and Noncount Nouns

Quantifiers are expressions of quantity that tell "how much" or "how many."

1. Use *a few, many / a lot of* with plural count nouns.

2. Use *a little, much / a lot of* with noncount nouns.

Incorrect:	~~a little~~ books	~~a few~~ money	~~much~~ people	~~many~~ homeworks
Correct:	a few books	a little money	many people	much homework

Remember: The phrase *a lot of* is correct with both count and noncount nouns.

Avoid using *much* in affirmative statements, even with noncount nouns.

Unusual:	We **have much** homework for tomorrow.
Correct:	We **do not have much** homework for tomorrow.
Better (informal):	We **have a lot of** homework for tomorrow.
Better (formal):	We **have a great deal of** homework for tomorrow.

Exercise 15 Read the sentences about numbers and languages. Underline the correct quantifier in each sentence. The first one has been done for you.

1. There are (<u>a few</u>, a little) Spanish speakers in my math class.

2. I don't know (many, a lot of) Spanish, so I can't speak to them.

3. In math class, the teacher asks us (many, much) questions about numbers.

4. Sometimes my Spanish-speaking classmates say the numbers in Spanish, so I have (a few, a little) opportunities to learn (a few, a little) Spanish.

5. (A few, A little) numbers are similar in English and Spanish. For example, *siete* looks like *seven* in my opinion.

6. However, (many, much) of the numbers are very different. For example, there is not (many, much) similarity between *cinco* in Spanish and *five* in English.

---

7. I asked my best friend about the best way to learn numbers in Spanish, but he did not give me (many, much) advice.

8. Perhaps if I do (a few, a lot of) homework in Spanish, that might help me to learn the numbers in Spanish.

3.8   Functions of Nouns in a Sentence

A noun can have three important functions in a sentence. A noun can be a **subject**, a **direct object**, or an **object of a preposition**.

subject:	**Mrs. Williams** is eighty years old.
direct object:	Because it was her birthday, we called **Mrs. Williams**.
object of a preposition:	I talked *about* **Mrs. Williams** with my family.

3.8.1   *Nouns as Subjects*

One function of a noun is the **subject** of a sentence. The subject of a sentence is the noun (or pronoun) that does the action of the verb. The subject can be a single word, such as *rock*, or a noun phrase. A noun phrase consists of a noun and all the words that go with it, such as *a heavy gray rock*.

Kangaroos *jump* incredibly high.

A **kangaroo** *has* a very special tail.

They *use* their long, heavy tails for balance.

To find the subject, first find the verb (the action word) in the sentence. Then ask: "Who" or "what" does the action of the verb? The answer will be the subject.

Kangaroos *jump* incredibly high.

Question:	What is the action word?
Answer:	**jump** = action = *verb*
Question:	Who or what jumps?
Answer:	**Kangaroos** = doer of action = *subject*

Exercise 16   Read these statements about animals. Then write a one-word answer to each question according to the statement. The first one has been done for you.

1. According to many scientists, dolphins communicate with each other.

   What is the action word? _____communicate_____ = verb

   Who or what does this action? _____dolphins_____ = subject

2. Elephants eat peanuts.

What is the action word? _____ = verb

Who or what does this action? _____ = subject

3. In both hot and cool weather, camels need a lot of water.

What is the action word? _____ = verb

Who or what does this action? _____ = subject

4. Alligators always live in areas near water.

What is the action word? _____ = verb

Who or what does this action?

_____ = subject

5. Raccoons often sleep in the daytime.

What is the action word?

_____ = verb

Who or what does this action?

_____ = subject

Exercise 17   Read the sentences about the two kinds of camels. Draw one line under the subject (doer of the action) and two lines under the verb. The first one has been done for you.

1. Of all the animals in the world, <u>camels</u> <u>are</u> certainly one of my favorite animals.

2. Camels are strange in several ways.

3. Camels live in desert areas.

4. A camel has extremely long

   eyelashes.

5. In my opinion, camels are beautiful

   animals.

6. To other people, camels are not so

   attractive.

Dromedary

7. Bactrian camels have two humps.

8. Dromedaries are camels with only one hump.

9. Dromedaries carry heavy supplies.

10. For these important reasons, people value camels very much.

Bactrian

Exercise 18 Read the sentences about cows. Write S over the subject and V over the verb. The first one has been done for you.

      S V
1. A cow is female.

2. A dairy cow provides milk.

3. Different kinds of cows produce different types of milk.

4. For example, Jersey cows give rich milk.

5. In contrast, Guernsey cows produce yellowish milk.

6. Cows vary in color.

7. A Holstein is black and white.

8. Most cows are quite gentle.

9. The average cow lives from nine to twelve years.

10. The average cow drinks thirty gallons of water every day.

3.8.2 Nouns as Direct Objects

A sentence often has a noun after the verb. This noun is called the **direct object**. The direct object tells who or what receives the action of the verb.

Monkeys *eat* **bananas**.

Question: What is the verb?

Answer: **eat** = action = *verb*

Question: Who or what eats?

Answer: **monkeys** = doer of action = *subject*

Question: What does the monkey eat?

Answer: **bananas** = receiver of action = *direct object*

Exercise 19 Read these sentences about writers and their writing. Then write a one-word answer to each question according to the statement. The first one has been done for you.

1. Writers choose their words very carefully.

    What is the action? _____choose_____ = verb

    Who / what does this action? _____writers_____ = subject

    Who / what receives the action? _____words_____ = direct object

2. Shakespeare wrote poetry.

    What is the action? _____ = verb

    Who / what does this action? _____ = subject

    Who / what receives the action? _____ = direct object

3. Ernest Hemingway authored many novels and short stories in his lifetime.

    What is the action? _____ = verb

    Who / what does this action? _____ = subject

    Who / what receives the action? _____ = direct object

4. Publishing companies print books.

    What is the action? _____ = verb

    Who / what does this action? _____ = subject

    Who / what receives the action? _____ = direct object

5. A newspaper company employs reporters and writers.

What is the action? _____ = verb

Who / what does this action? _____ = subject

Who / what receives the action? _____ = direct object

Exercise 20   Read the sentences about poetry in a student's reading class. Then write V above the verb, S above the subject, and DO above the direct object. The first one has been done for you.

         S   V   DO
1. At school, I enjoy my reading class the most.

2. I like reading for many good reasons.

3. In our reading class, we read many kinds of literature.

4. Right now we are reading Chapter 5 of our book.

5. Chapter 5 teaches some famous poems.

6. In class today, we read three different poems about nature.

7. The first poem tells the story of a young boy at the beach.

8. In the second poem, the woman saw the death of a young child.

9. The third poem discusses society's treatment of animals.

10. Reading poems gives me a very good feeling.

3.8.3   *Nouns as Objects of Prepositions*

The third function of a noun in a sentence is the **object of a preposition.** The object of a preposition is found within a prepositional phrase, which usually consists of a preposition and the words that go with it. (Some frequently used prepositions can be found in Chapter 6.)

Susan walked **to the supermarket in the morning.**
               PREP + OBJECT   PREP + OBJECT

A preposition may be followed by a noun or a pronoun and the words that go with it. The noun can be a concrete noun, an abstract noun, or a verb used as a noun (gerund).

I went **to** *the bank*. (bank = concrete noun)

I believe **in** *complete honesty*. (honesty = abstract noun)

I am in favor **of** *taking* a break now. (taking = verb used as noun = gerund)

I gave the money **to** *him* yesterday. (him = pronoun)

Exercise 21 Read these sentences about a TV show. Underline the prepositional phrases. There may be more than one in some sentences. The first one has been done for you.

1. My favorite show was <u>on television</u> last night.

2. The name of the show is "Pet Parade."

3. Pet Parade received very good ratings in the industry.

4. Most of the commercials for the show feature the crew's pets.

5. The crew members bring their pets to the studio two hours before show time.

6. For obvious reasons, most of the pets are very nervous during the shooting of the show.

Exercise 22 Write six sentences about the inside of a place such as your room, an office, a classroom, or a building. Each sentence should contain at least one prepositional phrase. Underline the prepositional phrases. Draw an arrow from the preposition to the object of the preposition. The first one has been done for you.

1. <u>On the wall</u> <u>of my bedroom</u>, there are four posters <u>with Japanese art</u>.

2. _____

_____

3. _____

_____

4. _____

_____

5. _____

_____

6. _____

_____

Exercise 23 Read these sentences about some friends who went to see a movie. Underline each noun. Write S for subject, DO for direct object, or OP for object of a preposition to indicate the function of each noun in the sentence. The first one has been done for you.

    S   OP   OP
1. <u>Helen</u> went to the <u>theater</u> at <u>noon</u>.

2. She waited for her two friends, but they did not arrive on time.

3. Helen entered the theater.

4. She found a seat.

5. Helen saved two seats for her friends.

6. Her friends were sitting behind a lady who was wearing a large red hat.

7. The woman was blocking the view of the other customers.

8. The woman did not know this situation.

9. The usher spoke to the woman.

10. After their discussion, the woman removed her hat.

11. As a result, Helen and her friends saw the movie.

12. At the end of the movie, the audience clapped wildly.

3.9 Possessive Forms of Nouns

There are two ways to show the possessive of nouns in English. One way is with **an apostrophe and the letter** *s* **(*'s*)**. The other way is with **the preposition** *of*. Consider the differences between these two possessive forms.

For people:

1. A singular noun that does not end in -*s:* add *'s*

    the boy has a book = the boy's book

    the boy has books = the boy's books

2. A plural noun that ends in -*s:* add *'* (apostrophe)

    the boys have one book = the boys' book

    the boys have many books = the boys' books

3. An irregular plural noun: add *'s*

    the children have a book = the children's book

    people have opinions = people's opinions

4. A name that ends in -*s:* add *'s*

    Chris has a laptop = Chris's laptop

    Charles has two bikes = Charles's bikes

For things:

5. Use *of* instead of *'s*

    a table has a top = **the top of** the table

    a book has a title = **the title of** the book

6. Exceptions: We use *'s* for time words and nature words

    Today's newspaper is on the table.

    The sun's rays provide us with warmth and vitamin D.

Exercise 24 Read the sentences about how parents, teachers, and administrators work together to help students. Underline each possessive noun and the noun that it describes. The first one is done for you.

1. Children try to work up to their <u>parents' expectations</u>.

2. Today's schools are trying to meet parents' and children's expectations.

3. Principals and teachers meet regularly for conferences with parents to discuss their

    children's progress.

4. Parent volunteers' input is invaluable because they observe students' interactions and habits.

5. The teachers' aides actually help students in the classroom, while parent volunteers'

   jobs may include recess and lunchroom duties.

Exercise 25   Write sentences about six famous people (a famous politician, a religious leader, a singer, an astronaut or scientist, an actor, a sports star). Use at least one possessive noun in each sentence. The first one has been done for you.

1. _Martha Washington was George Washington's wife._____

2. _____

3. _____

4. _____

5. _____

6. _____

Exercise 26   Write sentences using an "of" phrase to show possession in the following pairs of words. Circle the prepositional phrases. The first one has been done for you.

1. (color / house) _My brother does not like the color (of our house)._____

2. (tip / pencil) _____

_____

3. (door / car) _____

_____

4. (heel / shoe) _____

_____

5. (color / wallpaper) _____

_____

6. (taste / food) _____

_____

7. (smell / onion) _____

_____

8. (population / China) _____

_____

9. (feel / silk) _____

_____

10. (bottom / list) _____

_____

Exercise 27　Read the paragraph below. Rewrite it by making the eight changes listed. Careful: You may have to make other changes.

1. Make all nouns singular in the first five sentences and make all other necessary changes.

2. The word *animal* is used in the first three sentences. For variety, use the word *creature* in the second sentence.

3. In the fifth sentence, add the words *very hard* in the correct place.

4. Connect the two sentences about snails' food with the word *but*. Add a comma before the word *but*.

5. Use the word *or* to combine the two short sentences that talk about where a snail lives. Make a short sentence of just seven words.

6. Change *snails* to *snail* in the last sentence and make all necessary changes.

7. Begin the last sentence with the phrase *for these reasons*. Put a comma after this phrase.

8. In the last sentence, add the word *extremely* in the correct place.

All About Snails

　　I think that snails are the slowest animals on this planet. What do we know about these animals? Snails are small animals. They carry their houses wherever they go. Snails have shells to protect themselves. Most snails eat only plants. Some snails eat meat. Snails live in water. Snails live on land. Not many people know that more snails live in water than on land. I think that snails are interesting animals.

_____

_____

_____

(continued)

_____

_____

_____

_____

_____

_____

_____

_____

■ CHAPTER QUIZ

Exercise 28   **Part 1: Synthesis.** Circle the letter of the correct answer.

1. I can't watch this movie with you right now. My appointment is in _____ hour.

   A. a   C. an

   B. the   D. —

2. Lisa bought six new _____ .

   A. dress's   C. dress

   B. dresses   D. dress'

3. Those _____ have different _____ .

   A. baby ... birthday   C. babies ... birthday

   B. babys ... birthdays   D. babies ... birthdays

4. The babysitter watches the children carefully because they might hurt _____ .

   A. himself   C. themselfs

   B. themselves   D. himselfs

5. For most people, _____ honesty is the most important quality in a good friend.

   A. a   C. an

   B. the   D. —

6. _____ books do not cost _____ money.

   A. a little ... many   C. much ... a little

   B. many ... a few   D. a few ... much

Part 2: Error Correction. One of the four underlined words or phrases is not correct. Circle the letter of the error and correct it in the space provided.

7. I bought interesting biography at the small bookstore that is on Main Street.
    A   B   C   D

_____

8. Long-necked bird that is standing over there on one leg is a flamingo.
      A   B   C   D

_____

9. My brother's the best friend's home is next to the park on Peters Street.
     A   B   C   D

_____

10. Yesterday's newspaper carried an article about my favorite restaurant. It is at
      A   B
the top of the list because of the food's taste.
    C   D

_____

■ ORIGINAL WRITING

Exercise 29   On a separate sheet of paper, describe a gesture, such as snapping your fingers or bowing, that is used in both the United States and another country but has a different meaning. Explain how the meaning of the gesture changes from one place to another. Underline all the nouns.

4 Subject-Verb Agreement

Every sentence in English must contain a subject and a verb. In Chapter 3, you learned that subjects are the "doers" of the action. Subjects are followed by verbs. In Chapter 1, you learned that verbs are actions or states of being. The focus of this chapter is practicing agreement between the subject and the verb.

4.1 Subject-Verb Agreement: Present Tense Verbs

When you describe something using the simple present tense, the subject must agree with its verb in number (singular or plural) and person. You learned in Chapter 2 that with the simple present tense, verbs use an -*s*, -*es*, or -*ies* ending for the third person (he, she, it) singular.

Singular	Plural
I **ride** city buses.	We **ride** city buses.
You **ride** city buses.	You **ride** city buses.
My sister **rides** city buses.	My brother and my sister **ride** city buses.

Exercise 1   Read the sentences about a young man and his uncle. Circle the correct form of the words in parentheses. The first one has been done for you.

1. My uncle ((gives) / give) me advice

   regularly.

2. (His word / His words) contain important

   lessons.

3. He and I (talk / talks) on the phone and

   face to face.

4. I (goes / go) to his house every week.

5. Sometimes (we / he) go to a local bookstore.

6. The bookstore (overlooks / overlook) a small lake.

7. (The book in the shop / The books in the shop) come from all over the world.

8. (My uncle / My uncles) often gives me his own books to read.

9. After reading a book, my uncle and I (participates / participate) in interesting discussions.

10. (I / He) spend a lot of time with him.

Exercise 2   Read the sentences about the good points of a patio. In the blank, write the correct form of the verb in parentheses. The first one has been done for you.

1. Sheila (like) _____likes_____ the outdoors very much.

2. She (enjoy) _____ the beautiful patio of her apartment.

3. She and her roommate (spend) _____ a lot of time on the patio.

4. Sheila (use) _____ the patio for many things.

5. The patio (hold) _____ three lounge chairs and a barbeque.

6. Sheila and her roommate (like) _____ to grow vegetables.

7. Their tomato plant (grow) _____ best on the patio.

8. When the weather is nice, Sheila (cook) _____ hamburgers on the patio.

9. Sometimes they (study) _____ on the patio.

10. Sheila (sleep) _____ on the patio if the outside temperature is good.

Exercise 3   Choose a person you know, such as your best friend or a relative. Write five sentences about that person. Use the present tense.

Person: _____

1. _____

2. _____

3. _____

4. _____

5. _____

4.2 Subject-Verb Agreement: Negative Verbs

When you want to express a negative thought in the present tense, you must add the helping verb *do* or *does* (plus the negative *not*) to sentences that do not already have a helping verb.

Do not use *do* or *does* when the main verb is *be*.

Singular (positive):	My sister **rides** city buses.
Singular (negative):	My sister **does not ride** city buses.
Plural (positive):	My brothers **live** in New York City.
Plural (negative):	My brothers **do not live** in New York City.

When you use the third person singular in the negative, you must use *does not* (*doesn't*). All other forms use *do not* (*don't*).

In formal writing, it is best *not* to use contractions (*doesn't* or *don't*).

In the negative form, use *does*; never put *-s* on the main verb.

Incorrect:	My sister **does** not **rides** city buses.
Incorrect:	My sister do not rides city buses.
Incorrect:	My sister no rides city buses.
Correct:	My sister **does not ride** city buses.

Exercise 4　Read these sentences that describe a negative situation. Circle the correct form of the words in parentheses. The first one has been done for you.

1. I (doesn't understand / (don't understand)) the campus map.

2. (The handbook / The handbooks) don't explain the map very well.

3. The class (does not have / do not have) time to tour the campus.

4. My classmates (doesn't study / don't study) in the library.

5. (A used book / Used books) doesn't cost a lot of money in the bookstore.

6. (A dorm room / Dorm rooms) doesn't take much time to clean.

7. The cafeteria (doesn't serve / don't serve) steak.

8. My dorm room (doesn't have / don't have) a window.

9. Karen and Jeanette (doesn't go / don't go) to the gym on campus.

10. Ricardo (does not play / do not play) on the college basketball team.

Exercise 5   Read the sentences about my brother's job. If the sentence is positive, change it to negative. If the sentence is negative, change it to positive. Write your sentences in the blanks. The first one has been done for you.

1. My brother David likes his job.

    My brother David does not like his job.

2. His bosses don't bother him.

    _____

3. David's work interests him very much.

    _____

4. He learns new information every day.

    _____

5. David doesn't earn a lot of money at his job.

    _____

Exercise 6   Reread your sentences in Exercise 3, p. 80, about a friend or relative. Write five sentences about that same person. Use negative forms of verbs.

Person: _____

1. _____

2. _____

3. _____

4. _____

5. _____

4.3   Subject-Verb Agreement: With *be* (present tense)

Sentences that contain *be* in the present tense use the following forms:

Person	Singular	Plural
First	I **am** a college student.	We **are** college students.
Second	You **are** a college student.	You **are** college students.
Third	He **is** a college student.	They **are** college students.

Here are the forms for negative sentences:

Person	Singular	Plural
First	I **am not** a college student.	We **are not (aren't)** college students.
Second	You **are not (aren't)** a college student.	You **are not (aren't)** college students.
Third	He **is not (isn't)** a college student.	They **are not (aren't)** college students.

Exercise 7   Read the sentences about the beaches near Miami, Florida. Circle the correct form of the word in parentheses. The first one has been done for you.

1. The state of Florida ((is) / are) located in the

    southeastern part of the United States.

2. There (is / are) warm water on three sides

    of Florida.

Miami

3. For this reason, the weather in Florida (am / is / are) usually warm.

4. Miami (am / is / are) located in Florida.

5. Miami (is / is not) located in southern Florida.

6. Winters in Miami (is not / are not) cold.

7. One of the really nice beaches in Florida (is / are) Miami Beach.

8. Right now many people (is / are) swimming in the nice warm water at Miami Beach.

9. However, not everyone is in the water. Some people stay on the beach because they

    (is not / are not) good swimmers.

10. Because of the warm weather and great beaches, Florida (is / is not) a popular tourist

    destination.

Exercise 8   Choose a special place that you like. Using the present tense, write seven sentences about that place. Try to use both positive and negative verbs in your sentences.

Place: _____

1. _____

2. _____

3. _____

4. _____

5. _____

6. _____

7. _____

4.4 Subject-Verb Agreement: With *be* (past tense)

Sentences that contain *be* in the past tense use the following forms:

Person	Singular	Plural
First	<u>I</u> <u>was</u> in class yesterday.	<u>We</u> <u>were</u> in class yesterday.
Second	<u>You</u> <u>were</u> in class yesterday.	<u>You</u> <u>were</u> in class yesterday.
Third	<u>She</u> <u>was</u> in class yesterday.	<u>They</u> <u>were</u> in class yesterday.

Here are the forms for negative sentences:

Person	Singular	Plural
First	I **was not (wasn't)** in class yesterday.	We **were not (weren't)** in class yesterday.
Second	You **were not (weren't)** in class yesterday.	You **were not (weren't)** in class yesterday.
Third	She **was not (wasn't)** in class yesterday.	They **were not (weren't)** in class yesterday.

Exercise 9   Read the sentences about a sports fanatic. If the sentence is correct, write the letter C. If the sentence is not correct, write an X and make the necessary changes. The first two have been done for you.

_____C_____ 1. My friend Lisa loves to play sports.

_____X_____ 2. She enjoy*s* all types of sports, from team sports to individual sports like golf.

_____ 3. In fact, Lisa play on both the volleyball team and the golf team at our college.

_____ 4. She and her teammates practices every afternoon after classes.

_____ 5. Sometimes she travels out of town for tournaments, but she don't like

traveling because she misses a lot of class work.

_____ 6. Just last week, her team in North Carolina for a volleyball tournament.

_____ 7. Lisa a very good athlete.

_____ 8. She try her best in practice and during competitions.

Exercise 10   Rewrite the sentences from Exercise 9 as a paragraph. Indent the first line. (See p. 76 for an example of a paragraph with an indented first line.)

_____

_____

_____

_____

_____

_____

_____

_____

_____

_____

4.5   Subject-Verb Agreement: With Indefinite Pronouns

A pronoun usually replaces a specific noun. For example, you can use *she* instead of *my sister*. However, one group of pronouns does not refer to a specific noun. We call these **indefinite pronouns**. Examples of indefinite pronouns are *someone* and *everybody*.

On the next page is a list of common indefinite pronouns. Note that when indefinite pronouns are the subject of a sentence, they ALWAYS take a singular verb.

	every-	some-	any-	no-
-one	everyone	someone	anyone	no one
-body	everybody	somebody	anybody	nobody
-thing	everything	something	anything	nothing

Everybody *likes* our new teacher Dr. Olsen.

Something *smells* strange in the refrigerator.

Anyone *is* welcome to the party.

Exercise 11 Read the paragraph about life in New Mexico. There are seven errors in subject-verb agreement. Find and correct the errors. Hint: The numbers outside the box tell you how many errors are in each line.

Landlocked

1   My parents lives in New Mexico. They enjoy living there for a number of

1   reasons. First, the weather is predictable. The summer months is hot, but there is

little snow in the winter. New Mexico also has an interesting culture. Many types of

2   people live and works there. Everybody feel like New Mexicans. My parents are very

1   active, and New Mexico offer a lot of things to do. My father enjoys rock climbing,

1   and there are many places for him to practice this sport. My mother don't like the

beach, so New Mexico is perfect for her because it is a landlocked state. I love

1   visiting them in New Mexico. It are a lovely place to explore.

4.6 Subject + Prepositional Phrase + Verb

When the subject and the verb are separated by other words in a sentence, it can be difficult to make the subject and the verb agree. Sometimes subjects and verbs are separated by prepositional phrases (see Chapter 6) that give additional information about the subject. When you are writing, be sure to connect the subject and the verb even if additional words separate them.

The little **girl lives** on Hudson Street.
SUBJECT VERB

The little **girl** *in the blue and white sweater* **lives** on Hudson Street.
SUBJECT   PREPOSITIONAL PHRASE   VERB

The **houses** *near the supermarket* **are** not for sale.
SUBJECT PREPOSITIONAL PHRASE VERB

Some common prepositions include *in, near, at, on, to,* and *from*.

Exercise 12 Read the sentences. Underline the subject and circle the prepositional phrase. Then fill in the blank with the correct present tense verb. The first one has been done for you.

1. The computer (near the teacher's desk) (be) _____is_____ broken.

2. The laptop computer in the study lounge _____ (have, not) a lot

   of memory.

3. Those three computer books on top of the bookshelf _____

   (be, negative) mine.

4. The computer software in the language lab _____ (include)

   vocabulary and pronunciation practice.

5. The student behind me in class _____ (study, negative).

6. The computer lab across from the library _____ (contain) expensive

   computers.

7. My lab teacher from Switzerland _____ (speak) excellent Italian.

4.7   Subject-Verb Agreement: With *there + be*

When we want to explain that something exists, we use the form ***there + be***. The subject of the sentence is generally found after the verb *be*.

there + be + subject

Present tense: **There is** a huge *delay* on the highway right now.
              VERB   SUBJECT

              There are almost 300,000,000 *people* in the United States.
              VERB   SUBJECT

Past tense: **There were** five *concerts* at the amphitheater last weekend.
              VERB   SUBJECT

              There was a *problem* at work, so I had to stay late.
              VERB   SUBJECT

When using *there + be*, remember to find the subject and make sure that it agrees with the form of *be*.

Exercise 13   Read the sentences about studying psychology. Underline the subjects and draw two lines under the verbs. Hint: Some sentences may have more than one subject-verb combination. The first one has been done for you.

1. Psychology is an interesting field of study.

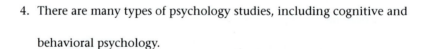

2. There are lots of students at the college who are psychology

   majors.

3. Students of this behavioral science like to study people's

   behaviors.

4. There are many types of psychology studies, including cognitive and

   behavioral psychology.

5. Psychology students learn many interesting things about people's behaviors.

6. One of my favorite psychology professors is Dr. Jamison.

7. There were two excellent psychology professors at the college, but they

   recently retired.

8. There are graduates of the psychology program who continue their studies in the

   master's program.

Exercise 14 Read the following paragraph. There are seven errors in subject-verb agreement. Find and correct the errors.

Advisers

If you doesn't know what to study in college, try talking to an academic adviser.

Advisers are great resources because they not require appointments. You can see

them two or three times a semester, and they happy to help you. There is many types

of advisers, from general studies advisers to specific subject advisers. The amount

of time you spend are up to you. Advisers are also good resources because they is

helpful and understanding. You can talk to them about many things, from academic

subjects to personal matters! Many students in college visits the advising office. Why

don't you try?

■ GUIDED WRITING

Exercise 15 Read the paragraph below. Rewrite it by making the eight changes listed. Careful! You may have to make other changes.

1. Change *John* to *John and Joanna.*

2. Change *one psychology major* to *three psychology majors.*

3. Change *good* to a stronger, more positive adjective.

4. Change the first *library* to *resource centers.*

5. The phrase *a lot of* is correct, but sometimes this phrase sounds like conversation instead of academic writing. Replace the second *a lot of* with the phrase *a great deal of.*

6. Insert the quantifier *thousands of* in front of the word *books.*

7. Change *two professors* to *a professor.*

8. Change the first verb in the last sentence to a negative form of the verb.

Student Life

John studies at the City College. He is interested in psychology and wants to become a psychologist. John is a sophomore, and this year he is choosing a major. There is one psychology major at the college, and it has a good reputation around the state. John spends a lot of time at the library. The library on campus contains a lot of information, including books, reference articles, and online databases. Because he doesn't have a job, John can concentrate on homework and research papers. John enjoys the classes at the college and studies as much as he can. In fact, there are two professors at the college that John likes. They always help John. John definitely wants to graduate because he loves school so much!

_____

_____

_____

_____

_____

_____

_____

_____

_____

_____

_____

_____

_____

Exercise 16   **Part 1: Synthesis.** Circle the letter of the correct answer.

1. No one in my office _____ our new boss. She gets angry very easily.

   A. are liking   C. like

   B. likes   D. is liking

2. _____ John still using the photocopier? I need to use it.

   A. Does   C. Are

   B. Did   D. Is

3. It may be true that a cat and a dog _____ usually play together, but my cat and dog get along just fine.

   A. don't   C. doesn't

   B. aren't   D. isn't

4. The new textbook that the school _____ for next semester costs over 100 dollars!

   A. chooses   C. has chosen

   B. choose   D. have chosen

5. Somebody _____ to water the plants. The leaves are turning yellow.

   A. are needing   C. need

   B. is needing   D. needs

6. How many people _____ to next weekend's party?

   A. do you invite   C. you invite

   B. did you invite   D. are you invite

Part 2: Error Correction. One of the four underlined words or phrases is not correct. Circle the letter of the error and correct it in the space provided.

7. I <u>started</u> to clean out my closet last night. Nothing that <u>is</u> in my closet <u>fit</u> me anymore.
      A   **B**   **C**
   I <u>need</u> to go shopping soon! _____
    D

8. There <u>is more</u> than 30 students in my English class. I <u>don't remember</u> anyone's name
      A   **B**
   there, and I <u>am sure</u> they <u>don't know</u> mine, either.
                 C   **D**

_____

9. <u>Mr. and Mrs. Brewster</u> knows the <u>whole neighborhood</u>, so if you <u>are</u> interested in
           A   **B**   **C**

   meeting your neighbors, you <u>need</u> to go visit the Brewster house.
                              D

   _____

10. I <u>have called</u> Bill's phone three times this morning. There <u>are</u> something wrong with
       A   **B**

    his phone, I <u>think</u>. It <u>is not working</u> today. _____
                 C   **D**

■ ORIGINAL WRITING

Exercise 17 On a separate sheet of paper, write an original paragraph (five to eight sentences) about an academic major that you are interested in. Discuss your interest in this major, including the necessary skills to be successful in this field of study. Focus on subject-verb agreement in your paragraph. Include sentences using the negative form and *there + be*. Underline all the subjects once and verbs twice and check to see that they agree.

*or
career field*

*Look for
comma rules
comma splices
S-V agreement*

5 Modals

In this chapter, you will study modals, which are words that express mood or tense and are used with verbs.

5.1 What Are Modals?

Modals are words that help main verbs by changing the meaning of the sentence. Modals are used to express:

5.2	requests and permission	**Can** you *stop* at the grocery store on the way home?
5.3	ability	When I was a child, I **could** *run* very fast.
5.4	necessity	International students **must** *have* a student visa in the United States.
5.5	possibility and probability	We **might** *go* to the beach this weekend.
5.6	advisability and suggestion	The lecturer **should** *speak* more clearly.

The most common modals are *can, could, may, might, should, would, ought to, must, have to,* and *be able to.* Remember that all modals are followed by the base form of the verb.

> I *ride* my bike to school. (This is something that I do every day.)

> I **may** *ride* my bike to school. (It is possible that I will ride my bike, or I may not. A second meaning is that I have permission [from my parents, for example] to ride my bike to school.)

> I **can** *ride* my bike to school. (I have the ability to ride.)

> I **must** *ride* my bike to school. (This is a necessity; I have no other transportation.)

Only use the base form of the verb after the modal.

Incorrect:	Margaret **will** ~~*to graduate*~~ next year.
Correct:	Margaret **will** *graduate* next year.
Incorrect:	The students **should** ~~*to study*~~ Chapter 7.
Correct:	The students **should** *study* Chapter 7.

Do *not* add *-s* to the base verb following a modal.

Incorrect:	He **can** *uses* the computer in the living room.
Correct:	He **can** *use* the computer in the living room.
Incorrect:	Lucille **would** *helps* if she had the time.
Correct:	Lucille **would** *help* if she had the time.

Some modals are combinations of more than one word. For these multiword modals, such as **be able to** and **have to**, you must change form according to the subject.

My dog **is able to** *jump* over the fence in the backyard.

We **have to** *change* the flat tire.

Do *not* use two one-word modals together in a sentence.

Incorrect:	You **may** ~~can~~ *eat* at my house.
Correct:	You **may** *eat* at my house. (permission – formal)

You **can** *eat* at my house. (permission – informal)

You can combine a one-word modal with a multiword modal.

I **may** **be able to** *help* you tomorrow.

We **might** **have to** *leave* the party early.

Exercise 1 Read these sentences about regional weather situations. Write M above the modal and V above the verb. The first one has been done for you.

 1. Weather can change very quickly.
 _M_ _V_

 2. Our weather channel has to give reports day and night.

 3. Weather patterns can be very diverse across the United States.

 4. It could be raining in Oregon and snowing in Illinois on the same day.

 5. People in the Midwest might see severe thunderstorms in May and June.

 6. Floridians should carry an umbrella with them in the summer.

 7. New Englanders ought to keep a snow shovel in the trunk of their cars.

8. Southern states should listen to hurricane warnings from June to October.

9. When there is a hurricane warning, some residents must evacuate.

10. When a resident has to leave his home, he could go to a safety shelter.

5.2　Modals for Requests and Permission

> can　could　would　may　might

When you use modals to ask for something, you politely **request**, or ask for **permission**.

CAN　informal

> **Can** I *use* your cell phone? (request)
>
> Joe **can** *go* next; I don't mind waiting. (permission)

COULD　informal

> **Could** you *close* the window? (request)
>
> You **could** *park* here. (permission)

WOULD　polite request

> **Would** you *like* to go to the movies tonight? (request)
>
> **Would** you *mind* if I sit here? (request for permission)

MAY　formal

> **May** I *have* your name, please? (request)
>
> You **may** *have* a seat. (permission)

MIGHT　very formal (not commonly used)

> **Might** I *offer* you a piece of candy? (request; not used for permission)

Requests are usually questions. The modal comes first in a question.

> **Can** I *have* some?

Do *not* use two one-word modals together in a sentence.

> *Incorrect:*　You **may** ~~can~~ *borrow* my car.
>
> *Correct:*　You **may** *borrow* my car. (permission – formal)
>
> 　　　　　You **can** *borrow* my car. (permission – informal)

Exercise 2   Read the two conversations. Fill in each blank using a modal of request or permission: *can, could, would, may, might*. Decide if the situation is formal or informal. The first one has been done for you.

Situation 1: A medical checkup

Doctor: Good morning, Mrs. Martine. How is Jack

today?

Mrs. Martine: Good morning, Dr. Wong. I'm afraid he's

not feeling well.

Doctor: May I hold him?

Mrs. Martine: Yes, you _____may_____. Please check his throat and ears.
1

Doctor: _____ you mind holding him in your lap so he won't be afraid?
2

You _____ want to distract him while I'm examining him. His
3

ears look fine, but his throat is red. I'm going to write a prescription for him. You

_____ want to fill this right away.
4

Mrs. Martine: Thank you very much.

Doctor: _____ our office call you tomorrow night to check on his progress?
5

Mrs. Martine: You certainly _____. Thanks again.
6

Doctor: You're welcome.

Situation 2: Two friends meeting at the supermarket

Sonya: Hi Christina. What a surprise to see you here! Are you in a hurry, or can we talk for a few minutes?

Christina: Hi Sonya. It's good to see you. I'm in kind of a hurry because I have to pick up my son from soccer practice.

_____ you mind if we set up something for tomorrow?
1

Sonya: If you are free tomorrow night, you _____ come to my house
2

for coffee.

Christina: My daughter has piano lessons tomorrow night. _____ we meet
3

in the daytime when the kids are in school?

Sonya: I _____ not come during the day because I'm teaching.
4

_____ we get together on Saturday?
5

Christina: That's a good idea. _____ you come to my house?
6

Sonya: Sure. What time?

Christina: Around noon?

Sonya: _____ I bring anything for lunch?
7

Christina: You _____ bring dessert.
                        8

Sonya: Great. See you on Saturday.

Christina: See you then.

Exercise 3   Write five sentences about a vacation you plan to take soon. Use the modals in parentheses. Write questions for at least two of the sentences.

1. (can) _____

_____

2. (may) _____

_____

3. (could) _____

_____

4. (might) _____

_____

5. (would) _____

_____

5.3   Modals of Ability

can   could (past ability)   be able to

These modals express **ability**. All three modals are followed by the base form of the main verb. Only *be able to* changes for third person singular. *Can* and *could* do *not* add *-s*.

CAN   ability

Harry **can *run*** faster than Jim.

COULD   ability, past tense

Carmen **could *recite*** the alphabet as a young child.

BE ABLE TO   have the ability to

I **am able to *drive*** without my glasses. (present)

Carol **is able to *drive*** without her glasses. (present – third person singular)

We **were not able to** *get* a reservation. (past, negative)

Peter **was able to** *make* the reservation. (past – third person singular)

Do *not* use two one-word modals in a sentence.

Incorrect:	I ~~can could~~ help you tomorrow.
Correct:	I <u>can</u> <u>help</u> you tomorrow. (ability)
Correct:	I <u>could</u> <u>help</u> you tomorrow. (possibility – different meaning)

Exercise 4   Read and complete the sentences with modals of ability: *can, could, am / is / are able to, was / were able to.* Be careful with third person singular. The first one has been done for you.

As an Adult:

1. I <u>can</u> <u>drive</u> a car.

2. I _____<u>can</u>_____ <u>eat</u> ice cream.

3. My brother and I <u>are able to</u> <u>stay out</u> late.

4. I _____ <u>ride</u> a bike.

5. I <u>am able to</u> <u>buy</u> a new computer.

6. I <u>can</u> <u>earn</u> a living.

7. I _____ <u>play</u> all day.

8. I <u>cannot</u> <u>fit</u> in a baby swing.

9. My brother and I _____

   <u>go</u> to college.

10. I _____ <u>ride</u> in a stroller.

As a Child:

I _____*could not*_____ <u>drive</u> a car.

I _____ <u>eat</u> ice cream.

We _____ <u>stay out</u> late

I _____ <u>ride</u> a bike.

I _____ <u>buy</u> one.

I _____ <u>earn</u> a living.

I <u>was able to</u> <u>play</u> all day.

I _____ <u>fit</u> in it.

We <u>were not able to</u> <u>go</u> to college.

I <u>could</u> <u>ride</u> in a stroller.

5.4 Modals of Necessity

must	have to	have got to	need to

Use these modals when something is required or **necessary**:

MUST   very strong

> Tomorrow is the final exam; everyone **must** *attend* class.

HAVE / HAS TO   used more often than *must*

> Luis **has to** *sell* his motorcycle before he buys a boat.

HAVE / HAS GOT TO (very informal)

> Anna is staying home from the party because she **has got to** *study.*

NEED TO   similar to HAVE / HAS TO

> I **need to** *get* a new pair of reading glasses.

Exercise 5   Read the conversation. Write M above the modals of necessity (*must, have to, have got to, need to*) and V above the verbs. The first one has been done for you.

> M   V
Sam: Henry, everybody from our class has to go to a special class with the professor today.

It's in the library.

Henry: I know. The professor is showing a documentary called "The Big Bang Theory."

I think it is going to be on our final exam.

Sam: Wow! This weather is awful! I'm sure that some of our classmates will be late because

of this rain.

Henry: We have got to do whatever we can so that everybody comes to see the movie.

Sam: Well, what can we do? Any suggestions?

Henry: Let's go to the library to see how many people are there, and maybe we can all come

up with a plan for the students who are not there yet.

Sam: The library is so far away! We've got to get there first.

Henry: There must be an easier way than walking across campus.

Sam: We could run to one building, walk through the first floor, and then run to the next building till we get there. That would keep us out of the rain some of the time.

Henry: OK. Let's do it.

Sam: This is hard! We're still so far away from the building!

Henry: Hey, there's Rosie in the golf cart.

Sam and Henry: Rosie, you have got to give us a ride! *Please!*

Rosie: Sure. Get in. Where are you going?

Sam and Henry: To the library. All twenty of us need to be there to see a movie.

Rosie: Oh, that's been canceled. Didn't you check your e-mail?

5.5 Modals of Possibility and Probability

| may | might | could | should | ought to | must | will | be going to |

Modals of **possibility** and **probability** indicate degrees, from a chance or possibility (50%) to definite (100%):

MAY / MIGHT / COULD 50% possibility

> It's short notice, but we **may / might / could** *go* to the concert on Friday if Steve gets tickets.

SHOULD / OUGHT TO better possibility

> Lori **should / ought to** *get* to class on time today because there is no traffic on the highway.

MUST almost certain (see Section 5.7 for more about negative modals)

> The football game is not sold out, so tickets **must** *be* available.

WILL / BE GOING TO definite

> Steve bought tickets, so we **will** *attend* / **are going to** *attend* the concert Friday night.

Exercise 6 Read this weather report. Write M above the modals of possibility (*may, might, could, should, ought to, must, will,* or *be going to*) and V above their verbs. The first one has been done for you.

Weather Summary

         M   V
Across the Southwest, there will not be a cloud in sight today.

California, Nevada, and Arizona are going to have a beautiful day.

The sun will shine all day long. In the South, Texas may also share

in some of that sunshine. There might be a few showers along the Gulf states. These

showers will move into the South. The South ought to feel damp throughout the day.

Tornado warnings are in place in the Midwest. Midwesterners

will definitely need to find refuge. Tornadoes may not last

long, but they cause a lot of damage. Thunderstorms may be

very severe, too. Residents must seek shelter for their own safety. In the Northeast,

Bostonians should stay indoors as well. A blizzard will hit the area tonight. By

tomorrow morning, there will be at least six inches of the "white

stuff" on the ground.

Exercise 7 Write a weather report for your city. Include the current weather and the forecast for the next few days. Underline the modals in your weather report.

_____

_____

_____

_____

_____

_____

_____

_____

_____

_____

_____

5.6   Modals of Advisability and Suggestion

| should | ought to | had better (threat) |

Use modals to give someone **advice or make a suggestion**:

SHOULD   advice or suggestion

> You **should** *take* an umbrella.

> You **shouldn't get** so angry; it was a mistake.

OUGHT TO   strong advice

> Dan **ought to take** the train because parking spaces are scarce.

HAD BETTER   warning or threat

> Michael **had better stop** smoking; otherwise, it could affect his health.

The negative form is *had better + not*.

> You **had better not** / You**'d better not** *do* that.

Exercise 8   Read the sentences about weather in Florida. Choose the correct modal of advice in parentheses and write it in the blank. The first one has been done for you.

1. In Florida, it usually rains every other day in August. If

   you plan to visit, you _____*should*_____ take an

   umbrella with you. (should, will)

2. In heavy rain, you _____ use the

   wipers on your car. (can, had better)

3. Some people come to Florida to play golf. However, as a safety precaution, you

   _____ avoid the golf course in a thunderstorm. (would, ought to)

4. If it starts raining, you _____ seek shelter. (had better, will)

5. Driving in heavy showers can be difficult. You _____ also keep a

   flashlight in your glove compartment. (can, should)

6. Of course you _____ keep extra batteries with your flashlight. (ought

   to, be able to)

7. In addition, you _____ also keep a cell phone and a portable radio

   handy. (can, should)

8. It does not rain every day, however. When you go to the beach on a sunny day, you

   _____ bring a bathing suit. (can, should)

9. If you decide to go swimming, you _____ pack a towel, too. (had

   better, would)

10. Sunglasses are something you _____ wear to protect your eyes from

    the bright sunlight. (will, ought to)

5.7   Negative Modals

In formal writing, negatives are formed by inserting DO / DOES + *not* before the verb. When you use a modal, *not* comes after the modal. Remember that in formal writing, contractions are not generally used.

> Paulo **could not** *find* Maria's phone number. (formal)
>
> Paulo **couldn't** *find* Maria's phone number. (informal)

Here are the negative modals:

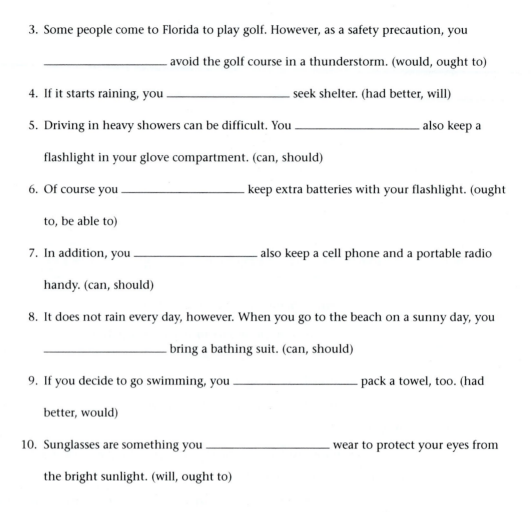

would + not = wouldn't

should + not = shouldn't

can + not = cannot = can't

may + not = may not (no contraction)

ought to + not = ought not
(no contraction)

be able to + not = am not able to
(no contraction), isn't, aren't, wasn't,
weren't able to

have to + not = do not have to = don't have to

has to + not = does not have to = doesn't have to

could + not = couldn't

will + not = won't

must + not = mustn't

might + not = might not
(usually not contracted)

1. When something is NOT NECESSARY, use *do not have to / doesn't have to / don't have to*.

   I feel a lot better. I **do not have to** *take* any more medication.

   The meeting was canceled; she **does not have to** *go.*

   You **don't have to** *shout;* I can hear just fine.

2. *Must + not (mustn't)* is used for prohibition (a very strong warning).

   Children **must not** *sit* close to the television. It will damage their eyesight.

   You **mustn't** *smoke* in restaurants in this state. Smoking in public places is against the law.

Exercise 9 Write the negative contractions for the following modals. If there is no contraction, write the full negative form. The first one has been done for you.

Negatives

1. should _____shouldn't_____ 6. might _____

2. must _____ 7. can _____

3. could _____ 8. ought to _____

4. may _____ 9. would _____

5. will _____ 10. is able to _____

Exercise 10 Think about the rules of your classroom. You may review your class syllabus if you have one. Write five sentences about what you can and cannot do in your class. Use *must, must not, should, should not,* and *ought to.*

1. _____

   _____

2. _____

   _____

3. _____

   _____

4. _____

   _____

5. _____

   _____

5.8 Questions with Modals: Review

Questions use inverted word order. Sentences with modals form questions by putting the modal first.

> I **can** *go* to the movies with you. / **Can** I *go* to the movies with you?

> John **was able to** *fix* his computer. / **Was** John **able to** *fix* his computer?

Do *not* use *do / does / did* with one-word modals in statements or questions.

Incorrect:	Sasha **does can** *drive* the car pool tomorrow.
Correct:	Sasha **can** *drive* the car pool tomorrow.
Incorrect:	**Do** you **should** *call* the doctor?
Correct:	**Should** you *call* the doctor?

Exercise 11 Read the pairs of sentences containing modals. Put a check mark next to the correct sentence. Pay special attention to the modals. The first one has been done for you.

Diet News

1. a. _____ You do should eat a balanced diet.

   b. ___✔___ You should eat a balanced diet.

2. a. _____ Fruits and vegetables can keep you healthy.

   b. _____ Fruits and vegetables can to keep you healthy.

3. a. _____ You must not taste vegetables while you are shopping.

   b. _____ You don't must not taste vegetables while you are shopping.

4. a. _____ A pepper may comes in red, green, or yellow.

   b. _____ A pepper may come in red, green, or yellow.

5. a. _____ Can you to eat the pit of an avocado?

   b. _____ Can you eat the pit of an avocado?

6. a. _____ You might have to wash the fruit first.

   b. _____ You might do have to wash the fruit first.

7. a. _____ The produce section of a grocery store may contain exotic

   fruits and vegetables.

   b. _____ The produce section of a grocery store may contains exotic

   fruits and vegetables.

8. a. _____ I should to go grocery shopping on Friday.

   b. _____ I should go grocery shopping on Friday.

9. a. _____ Could you would write a list for me?

   b. _____ Could you write a list for me?

10. a. _____ The store will to close at 9:00 p.m.

    b. _____ The store will close at 9:00 p.m.

■ GUIDED WRITING

Exercise 12   Read the paragraph below. Rewrite it by making the seven changes listed. Careful: You may have to make other changes.

1. Add *may* to the second sentence.
2. Change *a certain society* to plural.
3. Add *must* to the third sentence.
4. Change *the groom* to *the groom and his attendants* in the fifth sentence.
5. Change *usually* to *must* in the fifth sentence.
6. Insert *has to* after *father of the bride* in the sixth sentence.
7. In the last sentence, add *has to* after *sociologist.*

Sociology

   Sociology is the study of human behavior. A sociologist observes an institution such as marriage, religion, or education in a certain society. The sociologist pays close attention to food, clothing, and rituals because of the customs associated with them. For example, for a formal wedding in the United States, a bride must wear a long, white wedding gown and her attendants also wear formal gowns or dresses. The groom usually wears a tuxedo. Since the father of the bride walks his daughter down the aisle, he also wears a tuxedo. In keeping with the formality, the mothers of the bride and groom as well as the guests wear either formal or semi-formal outfits. Sociologists study not only the types of clothing but also the colors and materials. Different cultures give importance to different aspects. Therefore, a sociologist is a keen observer.

_____

_____

(continued)

_____
_____
_____
_____
_____
_____
_____
_____
_____
_____
_____
_____
_____
_____
_____
_____
_____
_____

■ CHAPTER QUIZ

Exercise 13   **Part 1: Synthesis.** Circle the letter of the correct answer.

1. If he has time, my boss _____ to the conference next week.

   A. may goes   C. might not go

   B. might goes   D. may go

2. The conductor _____ everyone's attention in order to start the symphony.

   A. has to has   C. have to has

   B. has to have   D. have to have

3. The professor _____ correct the exams by next Monday.

   A. should can   C. should be able to

   B. can should   D. can be able to

4. _____ you please close the window?

    A. Would   C. Should

    B. May   D. Must

5. Because he fell, the runner _____ finish the race.

    A. couldn't be able to   C. weren't be able to

    B. cannot   D. wasn't able to

6. When I was younger, I _____ run very fast.

    A. could   C. was able

    B. must   D. might

Part 2: Error Correction. One of the four underlined words or phrases is not correct. Circle the letter of the error and correct it in the space provided.

7. Paul's research paper is due next week, so he have to get to the library before it closes.
           A   B   C   D

_____

8. Since there's a storm warning, Jane has better check her flight before driving to
          A   B   C
the airport. _____
   D

9. We mayn't go to Jose's party tomorrow because we've already accepted an invitation to
      A   B   C
Maria's party. _____
   D

10. My car broke down last night. Can you able to give me a ride to class tomorrow
          A   B   C
morning? _____
   D

■ **ORIGINAL WRITING**

Exercise 14   On a separate sheet of paper, write an e-mail giving advice about the following situation: Your teenage daughter is visiting her cousin in another city. She sends you an e-mail to ask you for permission to go to the mall with her friends. You do not know the friends, and no parents will be present. You trust her to go to the mall, but you want to give her some parental advice. Give reasons why she should or should not do certain things. Underline all the modals.

6 *Prepositions*

Prepositions are small words, but they are perhaps the most difficult words to use correctly in a foreign language. There are many prepositions in English, but common English prepositions include *at, for, from, in, of, on, to.*

6.1 What Are Prepositions and Prepositional Phrases?

A **preposition** is a word that shows the relationship between a noun (or pronoun) and the rest of the sentence. Prepositions have many purposes, but they often give us information about place, time, and direction.

place:	**in** the classroom, **on** the table, **near** the bank, **at** the bank, **under** the table
time:	**in** the morning, **in** March, **in** 1985, **in** ten minutes, **for** ten minutes, **at** 9:45, **on** Monday
direction:	**to** the bank, **from** the bank

The combination of a preposition and its object (and any modifiers such as articles or adjectives) is called a **prepositional phrase**.

at home	under the sofa	on the green table
PREP + OBJ	PREP + ARTICLE + OBJ	PREP + ARTICLE + ADJECTIVE + OBJ

A **prepositional phrase** can come at the beginning, middle, or end of a sentence.

beginning:	**In central Canada,** the weather can be incredibly cold.
middle:	Vicky studied French **in central Canada** in 2005 and 2006.
end:	Dr. Ian Palmer teaches at a large university **in central Canada.**

Note that we usually use a comma after a prepositional phrase that comes at the beginning of a sentence.

beginning (with comma):	**In the last century,** air pollution damaged our forests.
end (with no comma):	Air pollution damaged our forests **in the last century.**

Exercise 1   Read the paragraph and underline the nine prepositional phrases. Circle the prepositions. Add commas to separate introductory phrases from the subject of the sentence. The first one has been done for you.

Population

(Of) all the countries in the world the United States ranks third in population

after China and India. The population of the United States is approximately

300,000,000. In the United States the state with the most people is California. Other

U.S. states that have large populations include Texas, New York, Florida, and Illinois.

The state with the smallest number of people is Wyoming.

Exercise 2   Use each preposition to create a prepositional phrase in a sentence about yourself. Circle the preposition. Underline the object of the preposition. Put some of the prepositional phrases at the beginning of your sentences. The first one has been suggested for you.

1. from _I drive (from) my home to school every morning._____

2. with _____

3. in _____

4. at _____

5. on _____

6. about _____

7. for _____

8. of _____

6.2   40 Common Prepositions

about   This book is **about** a cat and a dog.

above   There is a cloud **above** the mountain.

across   I am going to swim **across** the lake.

after   If you arrive **after** 6:00 p.m., there might not be any more food.

against   We are **against** the president's plan to raise taxes.

along   Yellow flowers grow **along** the river.

around   The dog ran **around** the tree several times.

---

as	For Halloween, she dressed up **as** a clown.
at (+ place)	The hotel is **at** 330 Wilson Avenue.
(+ time)	Flight 62 from Buenos Aires arrives **at** 9:37 p.m.
before	I came home **before** midnight.
behind	The cat is sleeping **behind** the car.
below	The temperature last night dropped **below** 32 degrees!
beside	My apartment building is **beside** the highway.
between	I'm sitting **between** Jose and Chen.
by (+ time)	You must complete this assignment **by** tomorrow.
(+ -*self*)	Do you live **by** yourself?
(+ place)	The museum is located **by** a park and a lake.
despite	We went to the beach **despite** the cloudy weather.
down	The truck rolled **down** the embankment.
during	**During** his entire vacation, Mike had a terrible cold.
except	I like all animals **except** snakes and lizards.
for (+ person)	This present is **for** you.
(+ period)	We stayed in Toronto **for** five days.
from	This semester lasts **from** January to May.
in (+ place)	Trenton is **in** New Jersey.
(+ time)	Halloween is **in** October.
(+ period)	Please come back **in** twenty minutes.
in back of	I think your book is **in back of** the computer.
in front of	I can't find my keys. They were **in front of** the computer.
in spite of	We went to the beach **in spite of** the cloudy weather.
instead of	Can you bring me some tea **instead of** coffee?
like	I think that turkey tastes **like** chicken.
near	**Near** the library, there is a large parking lot.
next to	Nevada is **next to** California.
of	What is the name **of** your professor?
off	You should take your hat **off** your head when you enter a building.
on (+ surface)	There are two maps **on** the classroom wall.
(+ street)	My house is **on** Glenwood Drive.
since	My wife and I have lived here **since** 1998.
through	Suddenly a bird flew **through** the window.
to	I'm going **to** the library now.
under	Your notebook is **under** the computer.

until	The class begins at 9:00 a.m. and lasts **until** 10:30 a.m.
up	Be careful when you walk **up** the stairs.
with	Please write your answers **with** a blue or black pen.
without	Many students prefer a book **without** long explanations.

Exercise 3 Some people are good with kids, but others are not so good with them. Read the sentences about Katie and children. Underline the correct preposition in parentheses. The first one has been done for you.

1. Katie loves kids, so she works (<u>at</u>, until) a day care center.

2. She goes (at, to) the day care center (in, at) 8:00 a.m every day.

3. The center is open (from, under) Monday (around, to) Friday, five days a week.

4. The children usually arrive (about, behind) 8:30 or 9:00.

5. Katie works with twenty children, so the job is not always easy (for, from) her.

6. (Down, During) play time, there are children everywhere.

7. Children often hide from Katie (in, under) the tables.

8. One little boy always tries to climb (down, on) top of the bookshelf.

9. One time he almost fell (around, off) the table. He's a very active child!

10. In addition, the day care center is (in, near) a busy street, so Katie has to be attentive.

11. (At, For) the end of the day, Katie is usually tired.

12. After a long work week, Katie loves to go out (against, with) her friends.

Exercise 4 Read the sentences about Katie and her weekends. Underline the correct preposition in parentheses. The first one has been done for you.

1. Like most young people, Katie likes to have fun (in, <u>on</u>) the weekend.

2. (After, From) being around little kids all week, Katie enjoys seeing people her own age.

3. Going out is more fun if you go (with, up) your good friends.

4. Katie and her friends usually go out to the club (at, in) 10:00 p.m.

5. Katie has a car and usually drives her friends (at, to) the club.

6. Their favorite club is downtown. It's really a great place to go (in, on) Saturdays.

7. (In spite of, In back of) working very hard all week, Katie manages to save a little

   energy for the dance floor.

8. The club stays open (for, until) 4:00 a.m., but Katie never stays (for, until) closing time.

9. Katie and her friends usually leave the club (on, before) 2:00 a.m.

10. She loves to laugh with her friends (to, about) all the funny people they meet during the night.

11. In fact, some of the people Katie meets behave exactly (like, for) some of the children at the day care center.

12. Some people enjoy life. These people try to have fun all (of, with) the time.

6.3 Describing Place and Time with *at, on, in*

Three prepositions that cause a lot of problems are **at, on,** and **in**. These three prepositions have many different uses, but there is an easy way to remember some of them. Study the diagram and the charts below.

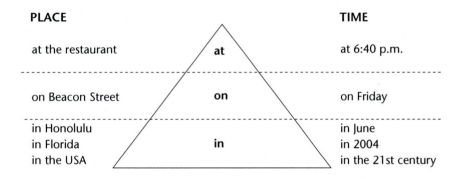

PLACE		TIME
at the restaurant	**at**	at 6:40 p.m.
on Beacon Street	**on**	on Friday
in Honolulu in Florida in the USA	**in**	in June in 2004 in the 21st century

	PLACES	TIMES
	very specific place, especially with the name of the place	very specific time; clock time
AT	**at** Jefferson Community College	**at** 10:17 a.m.
	at the Hilton	**at** noon
	at Pizza Hut	**at** midnight

	STREETS	DAYS
ON	**on** Kennedy Avenue	**on** Monday
	on Smith Street	**on** June 17
	on Interstate 10	**on** my birthday

	LARGE PLACES	LARGE TIME PERIODS
IN	**in** my neighborhood	**in** these two weeks
	in Chicago	**in** October
	in Illinois	**in** spring
	in the Northeast	**in** the 1970s
	in North America	**in** the 18th century

Exception with the parts of a day:

in the morning, **in** the afternoon, **in** the evening, **at** night

Exercise 5 Fill in the blanks with the correct preposition (*at, in,* or *on*) for these places and times. Then in the parentheses, write *place* or *time*. The first one has been done for you.

1. __in__   (____place____) South America

2. _____   (_____) the same year

3. _____   (_____) Hoover High School

4. _____   (_____) 1983

5. _____   (_____) April

6. _____   (_____) April 15

7. _____   (_____) April 15, 1983

8. _____   (_____) winter

9. _____   (_____) Miami

10. _____   (_____) sunrise

11. _____   (_____) the morning

12. _____   (_____) Senegal

13. _____   (_____) the Northern Hemisphere

14. _____   (_____) Disney World

15. _____   (_____) Wilson Road

16. _____   (_____) Africa

17. _____   (_____) your neighborhood

18. _____   (_____) Labor Day

19. _____   (_____) the M iddle East

20. _____ (_____) Guatemala and Mexico

21. _____ (_____) dawn

22. _____ (_____) Los Angeles

23. _____ (_____) Los Angeles International Airport

24. _____ (_____) California

Exercise 6   Read these sentences about Jeremy's life. Complete the sentences with *in, at,* or *on.* The first one has been done for you.

1. Jeremy was born ___in___ a small town ___in___ Georgia ___on___ April 1, 1980.

2. He lived _____ the same small house _____ the same little town all of his life until he went away to university.

3. Jeremy's favorite class _____ the university is geography. He loves to look at the globe and think about all of the different places _____ the world where people live.

4. The United States is located _____ the northern hemisphere, and Georgia is _____ the southeastern part of the United States.

5. The town where Jeremy was born is so small that it isn't even _____ the map.

6. Some people think geography is boring, but not Jeremy. There are a lot of interesting websites _____ the Internet, and _____ TV there is a program _____ the National Geographic Channel about ancient mapmakers that Jeremy watches _____ Friday nights _____ 10:00.

7. Most people do not realize this: _____ North America, the summer is _____ June, July, and August, but _____ South America, the summer is _____ December, January, and February. That's pretty interesting.

8. New York City and Santiago, Chile are _____ the same time zone, but when it's daytime _____ North and South America, it's nighttime _____ China.

9. There are so many places to go and so many things to do: see Carnival _____ Brazil, scuba dive in the Great Coral Reef _____ Australia, ride a gondola _____ Venice, fall in love _____ Paris, ride a camel to the pyramids _____ Egypt.

10. Jeremy cannot wait to finish his studies _____ the university this summer and

move away from the little house, _____ the same little street, _____ the same

little town where he's lived all his life. _____ graduation day, he plans to open up a

map of the world, close his eyes and put his finger down somewhere, anywhere in the

world and go.

Exercise 7 Read the paragraph about Dr. Marie Curie. Find and correct the five errors with the prepositions *at, on,* and *in.* The first one has been done for you.

Dr. Marie Curie

Dr. Marie Curie was one of the

most famous scientists of the twentieth

century. She is known to the world for

her discovery of the radioactive elements

radium and polonium.

Marie Curie was born Maria

Sklodowska ~~at~~ Warsaw, Poland, in
      ^in

November 7, 1876. Even from a very early age, it was obvious that Marie was an

exceptional child. She was able to read fluently by the time she was four years old and

amazed her family with her incredible memory. In 1891, in the age of fifteen, Marie

began studying chemistry and physics in the Sorbonne University in Paris. In 1901,

Marie was awarded the Nobel Prize in Physics for identifying two previously unknown

(continued)

elements. Only ten years after winning the first Nobel Prize, Marie was honored with a

second Nobel Prize in 1911, this time in chemistry. Marie Curie was the first person in

history to ever receive this honor twice.

However, because of her repeated exposure to radioactive materials, Marie

Curie died of leukemia on 1934. Through her life's work, Marie Curie made valuable

contributions to the field of science and to our understanding of radioactive elements.

6.3.1   *Idiomatic Expressions with* at, on, in

Here are some **idiomatic** uses of prepositions of location that you may need to memorize.

IN vs ON:	**in** bed (sleeping)	**on** the bed (sitting)
AT vs IN:	**at** the hospital (visiting, working)	**in** the hospital (a patient)
	at the school (visiting, working)	**in** school (a student)
AT:	**at** home	
	at work	
IN:	**in** class	

Exercise 8   Read the paragraph about a gift. Circle the correct preposition in parentheses. The first one has been done for you.

The Gift

One of my first memories was when I was six years old and fell out of a tree.

I hit my head pretty badly, and I was (at, (in)) the hospital for a week. I had to stay
               1

(in, on) bed for several days, which was pretty boring for a six-year-old. Fortunately,
 2

my uncle worked (at, in) the same hospital, so he would come and see me whenever
        3

my parents had to work. One morning I woke up and found a Nintendo sitting

---

(continued)

(in, on) the bed next to me. That was what I remember the most! I didn't have a
4

Nintendo (at, at the) home, and I was very excited about getting one. That is when I
5

realized that being (at, in) the hospital and playing video games all day is not so bad
6

after all. It was certainly more fun than being (at, in) class.
7

6.3.2 *Different Meanings for* at, in, *and* on

1. Sometimes the meaning of a preposition is easy to understand.

   The clerk put the shirt **in** *a white box.* The box is **on** *the table.*

In this example, *in* means *inside something* and *on* means *on top of something.*

   My cousin works at Washington Bank. He works in the Accounting Department.

In this example, *at* means *at a specific location* and *in* means *in a larger unit* (for example, a department or an office).

2. Sometimes the meaning of a preposition is not clear.

   I bought my car **in** *2005.* I bought my car **on** *my birthday.*

Why do we say *in 2005* and not *on 2005*? Why do we say *on my birthday* and not *in my birthday*? (Answer: We use *in* with years and *on* with dates.)

Exercise 9 Think of five examples of prepositions that confuse you. Write sentences with those prepositions here. Circle the prepositions that are difficult for you to understand.

1. _____

2. _____

3. _____

4. _____

5. _____

6.4 Prepositions of Time

Prepositions can introduce time phrases. For example, we use *at* with specific times (*at 6:45 p.m.*), and we use *since* to tell the beginning of a time period (*since 1992*).

Here are some common prepositions of time.

after	between	for	on	to
at	by	from	past	till
before	during	in	since	until

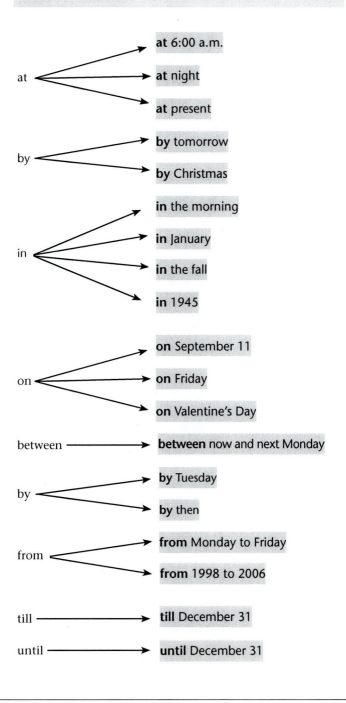

We use *for* with a general period of time and we use *during* with the name of a period of time. We use *for* to answer the question *How long?* and we use *during* to answer the question *When?*

Incorrect:	They visited France ~~during~~ two weeks.
Correct:	They visited France **for** two weeks.
Correct:	They visited France **during** the summer.

Exercise 10 Read the e-mail message about an upcoming visit. Underline the correct prepositions in parentheses. The first one has been done for you.

> Pablo,
>
> Hi, Bill here . . . I'm writing to let you know my schedule
>
> for when I visit your office next week. I have a lot to do
>
> (<u>between</u>, from, on) now and then, so I'm sending you my
>   **1**
>
> information now. (By, During, From) our last phone conversation,
>   **2**
>
> you told me to send you my information a.s.a.p. Well, here it is.
>
> My flight arrives (around, between, until) 11:00 a.m., and
>   **3**
>
> (at, by, past) the time I get out of the airport and get a rental car,
> **4**
>
> I should be at your office just (after, from, to) noon. This means
>   **5**
>
> that we will not see each other (at, from, in) the morning, so all of
>   **6**
>
> our work has to be done (at, in, since) the afternoon. I hope that
>   **7**
>
> we can have at least three hours to ourselves. Perhaps we can work
>
> (after, from, until) 1:00 (by, on, till) 4:00. What do you think?
> **8**   **9**
>
> I hope we can accomplish a lot (for, during) these three hours.
>   **10**

(continued)

```
        Maybe I can meet with your supervisor (at, in, on) 4:00 or
                                                    11

4:30. Do you think this is possible? Let me know. I haven't seen


him (for, during) a really long time.
         12

    Bill
```

Exercise 11   Write at least six sentences (or a short paragraph) about how you spend a typical day. Use at least six prepositions of time. Circle the prepositions.

_____

_____

_____

_____

_____

_____

_____

_____

Exercise 12   Here is a weekly schedule. Fill in some of the daily activities from your routine. Then choose eight activities from the schedule and write sentences about them. Use prepositions of time (*at, by, in, on, between, from, till, until*). A few ideas have been suggested for you.

	Mon	Tues	Wed	Thurs	Fri	Sat	Sun
8:00	Wake up						
9:00		Have breakfast					
10:00	Have class	Go to the library	Have class	Work in the school mailroom	Have class		

1. _I have class at 10:00 on some weekdays._ _____

2. _____

_____

3. _____

_____

4. _____

_____

5. _____

_____

6. _____

_____

7. _____

_____

8. _____

_____

Prepositions of Length of Time

The prepositions *for, since*, and *during* indicate a **period of time**.

FOR   Use with a quantity, or period, of time.

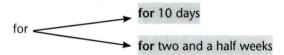

for ⟶ **for** 10 days

⟶ **for** two and a half weeks

SINCE   Use with the exact beginning of a period of time.

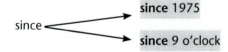

since ⟶ **since** 1975

⟶ **since** 9 o'clock

DURING   Use with the name of a period of time.

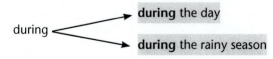

during ⟶ **during** the day

⟶ **during** the rainy season

In English, "a half" comes before the time word. We say "five and a half hours," not "five hours and a half."

Exercise 13   Read the sentences about a trip to Spain. Six of them contain an error with *for, since*, and *during*. Find the errors and correct them. The first one has been done for you.

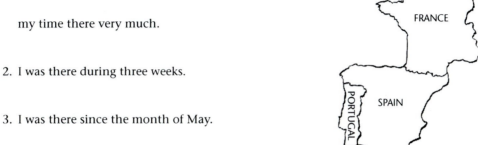

1. I went to Spain ~~since~~ *for* my last vacation. I enjoyed

   my time there very much.

2. I was there during three weeks.

3. I was there since the month of May.

4. During the time I was there, the weather was hot.

5. When I was there, I studied in a Spanish language program for six hours every day.

6. Unfortunately, I have not practiced my Spanish since I came back from Spain.

7. I would really like to return to Spain, but I want to stay during a longer period of time.

8. My cousin is in Spain now. He has been there for last month.

9. My cousin will stay there for a total of two months.

10. I will not visit him there for that time.

6.5 Prepositions of Direction or Movement

These prepositions indicate a movement in a direction or a specific direction.

arrive **in** a city, state, or country

arrive **at** a place (restaurant, school, work)

go **to** a city, state, country, place

go **from** a place

Do not make these common errors:

	Incorrect	Correct
enter + place:	She entered **in** the room.	She entered the room.
go + *to* + place:	She went the class.	She went **to** the class.
leave + place:	I will leave **from** the club.	I will leave the club.
return + *to* + place:	They returned their country.	They returned **to** their country.

The word *home* does not use a preposition with verbs of motion.

Incorrect: What time did you return **to** home?

Correct: What time did you return **home**?

Exercise 14   Read the paragraph about a trip to a foreign country. Find the eight mistakes in prepositions of direction or movement and correct them. The first one has been done for you.

Abroad

Few activities are more eye-opening and educational than traveling abroad.

When you go from your native country ~~for~~ *to* another country, there are so many new

things to see and experience. After you arrive in the airport, a good idea is to ask a

taxi driver to suggest some local favorite attractions. The mistake that most people

make when they arrive at the new country is to look for familiar things. Enjoy the

differences. Why, for example, would you want to go a fast food restaurant and eat

a hamburger when you can do that any day in your home town? Try some delicious

traditional cuisine instead. Here is a hint: if you already recognize every item on the

menu, don't even enter in the restaurant. Go to the places where you find mostly

local people. Another travel tip is to try walking when you have to go for one place

---

(continued)

to another. Cars are faster, but you see more on foot. By taking in some of the native

sights and sounds, when you leave from the new country and go back to home, you

will have some new memories to treasure.

6.6 Prepositions in Combination

Prepositions can be used to indicate place, time, and direction. In addition, prepositions can be used with certain nouns, verbs, and adjectives. You need to memorize these combinations and practice them in your writing and conversation.

6.6.1 Prepositions and Nouns

Some prepositions are used before certain nouns: **in** trouble
Some prepositions are used after certain nouns: a question **about**

There is no rule to explain these combinations. You must memorize them.

Preposition + Noun

at	**at** home	**at** present	**at** war	**at** work	
in	**in** a hurry	**in** danger	**in** debt	**in** love	**in** shape **in** trouble
on	**on** vacation	**on** sale	**on** your mind		

Noun + Preposition

about	confusion **about**	a question **about**	
in	experience **in**	an interest **in**	
for	an excuse **for**	a need **for**	a reason **for**
of	take advantage **of**	the middle **of**	
with	experience **with**	a problem **with**	
to	answer **to**	a decision **to**	

If you use a verb form after a preposition, the verb must end in *-ing*. (This form is called a gerund, which is a verb form used as a noun. Here it is an object of the preposition.)

Incorrect: Do you have any interest **in** *go* to the lake with us on Saturday?

Incorrect: Do you have any interest **in** *to go* to the lake with us on Saturday?

Correct: Do you have any interest **in** *going* to the lake with us on Saturday?

Exercise 15   Underline the correct preposition. The first one has been done for you.

1. (<u>on</u>, to) sale
2. a reason (at, for)
3. a decision (of, to)
4. (at, for) present
5. take advantage (of, with)
6. a question (about, at)

7. (for, in) danger
8. an answer (of, to)
9. an excuse (for, with)
10. (at, in) war
11. (at, in) a hurry
12. confusion (about, for)

13. experience (on, with)
14. (at, in) love
15. (at, in) work
16. (in, on) vacation
17. a problem (for, with)
18. (in, on) your mind

Exercise 16   Fill in the correct preposition with the noun. Then use each phrase to write an original sentence about Kevin, an imaginary bad student. The first one has been done for you.

1. an excuse _____for_____ : Kevin is always late. There is no excuse for being late.

2. have an interest _____ : _____

_____

3. take advantage _____ : _____

_____

4. have a problem _____ : _____

_____

5. give a reason _____ : _____

_____

6. agree with the decision _____ : _____

_____

7. have a need _____ : _____

_____

8. was some confusion _____ : _____

_____

6.6.2 Prepositions and Verbs

Some prepositions are used after certain verbs: listen to, wait for, complain about

You must memorize these verb and preposition combinations.

Incorrect:	I **complained** the homework. (Problem: no preposition)
Incorrect:	I **complained for** the homework. (Problem: wrong preposition)
Correct:	I **complained** about the homework.

If you use a verb form after a preposition, the verb must end in *-ing*. (This form is called a gerund, which is a verb form used as a noun. Here it is an object of the preposition.)

Incorrect:	I complained **about** *do* the homework.
Correct:	I complained **about** *doing* the homework.

Here are some common preposition and verb combinations.

verb + *about*	verb + *for*	verb + *to*	verb + *with*
ask **about**	apologize **for**	agree **to**	agree **with**
complain **about**	ask **for**	be accustomed **to**	argue **with**
dream **about**	look **for**	be used **to**	disagree **with**
forget **about**	study **for**	belong **to**	
talk **about**	thank (someone) **for**	explain (something) **to**	
think **about**		give **to**	
worry **about**	**verb + *on***	introduce **to**	
	count **on**	listen **to**	
verb + *at*	depend **on**	look forward **to**	
laugh **at**	keep **on**	pay attention **to**	
look **at**		speak **to**	

Exercise 17 Read the sentences about a special gift that Mark received. Locate the verb and preposition combinations. Draw two lines under the verb and circle the preposition that goes with that verb. The first one has been done for you.

1. Mark had a great surprise yesterday

   when his grandmother gave a computer

   (to) him because it was his birthday.

2. Mark thanked his grandmother for

   the great gift that she gave him for his

   birthday.

Prepositions in Combination   129

3. For a long time, Mark had dreamed about getting a computer, so he was extremely happy.

4. At first, Mark's grandmother thought about a gift card from a store.

5. However, she changed her mind because one day she saw Mark looking at computers in a newspaper advertisement.

6. She spoke to Mark about why he wanted a computer.

7. Mark thought about her question, and then they discussed his reasons.

8. Mark was impressed that his grandmother spent at least an hour with him and listened to his reasons.

9. Mark explained that most students today depend on computers to help them with their homework.

10. Mark's grandmother agreed with him that computers are important for school.

11. In addition, Mark explained that most of his friends had their own computers, so he looked forward to having his own computer.

12. Mark can never again complain about not having a computer.

Exercise 18   Fill in the correct preposition with the verb. Then write an original sentence with each phrase. The first one has been done for you.

1. be accustomed ____to____ : _I am accustomed to sleeping late on Saturdays._

2. agree _____ : _____

_____

3. count _____ : _____

_____

4. forget _____ : _____

_____

5. argue _____ : _____

_____

6. worry _____ : _____

_____

7. thank _____ : _____

_____

8. belong _____ : _____

_____

Prepositions and Adjectives

Some prepositions are used after certain adjectives: excited **about**

You must memorize these preposition and adjective combinations.

adjective + *of*	**adjective +** *by*	**adjective +** *for*	**adjective +** *with*
afraid **of**	bored **by / with**	bad **for**	all right **with**
guilty **of**	embarrassed **by**	good **for**	familiar **with**
proud **of**	frustrated **by / with**	ready **for**	O.K. **with**
sure **of**		necessary **for**	pleased **with**
tired **of**	**adjective +** *to*		satisfied **with**
	confusing **to**		
	important **to**	**adjective +** *from*	
adjective + *about*	married **to**	different **from**	
angry **about / at**	opposed **to**	divorced **from**	
concerned **about**	related **to**		
excited **about**		**adjective +** *in*	
happy **about / with**	similar **to**	disappointed **in / with**	
sorry **about / for**		interested **in**	
worried **about**			

One of the most common errors is using the preposition *for* too often.

Incorrect: We are happy ~~for~~ the professor's decision.

Correct: We are happy **about** the professor's decision.

If you use a verb form after a preposition, the verb must end in *-ing*. (This form is called a gerund, which is a verb form used as a noun. Here it is an object of the preposition.)

Incorrect: We are worried **about** ~~fly~~ to New York in January.

Correct: We are worried **about flying** to New York in January.

Exercise 19   Use these adjectives with the correct preposition combination to write original sentences about yourself. Remember to use a gerund (verb ending in *-ing*) if you use a verb after the preposition.

1. interested _____

_____

2. tired _____

_____

3. ready _____

_____

4. satisfied _____

_____

5. excited _____

_____

6. afraid _____

_____

7. worried _____

_____

8. similar _____

_____

9. happy _____

_____

10. frustrated _____

_____

11. different _____

_____

12. opposed _____

_____

Exercise 20   Read the letter from a student to her professor. Find the twelve errors with prepositions and correct them.

> Dear Professor:
>
> Tomorrow my English class starts, and I am excited for that. I have a question for my son. My son is 15 years old. He is in vacation here at the United States now, but he has to return Peru on February. He will be here during only a short time, and I would like to invite him to our class. Is this all right for you?
>
> If you agree for this plan, I will tell him. He speaks a little English, but he needs to practice more. I think this class is good for him. Is that possible? If you say it is okay, he will come the class with me tomorrow.
>
> I want to thank to you for your help. I am so happy for this wonderful opportunity for my son and myself.
>
> Sincerely,
>
> Ana Fernandez

■ GUIDED WRITING

Exercise 21   Read the paragraph below. Rewrite it by making the eleven changes listed. Careful: You may have to make other changes, including adding prepositions and changing verb forms.

1. Change all contractions to their full forms.
2. Add *this idea* to the second sentence.
3. Add *hear* to the third sentence.
4. Connect the two sentences that talk about *my life*.

5. There are two sentences about the writer's father and two sentences about the writer's mother. Add two more sentences about another family member. Follow the writer's pattern of a statement and a question. In your statement, use the word *frustrated*.

6. Add the adjective *current* in front of the word *questions*.

7. Add a verb form after the phrase *interested in*.

8. Add an adjective in front of the word *English* in the third to last sentence. Use an adjective that has a negative meaning.

9. Change the word *soon* to *May*.

10. After the word *ready*, add the phrase *whatever life brings me*.

11. Give your new paragraph a good title. Your title should represent the main idea of the whole paragraph, not just one specific idea.

I am a student, so people tell me all the time how lucky I am because I don't have any problems. I disagree. I'm tired of this opinion. My life is not so simple. My life is not so carefree. I think about my family all the time. I am worried about my father. Will he keep his job? I'm concerned about my mother. Will she remember to take her medicine? I also worry about school. Will I pass my classes? Will I really improve my English? When will I be able to understand native speakers? In addition to these questions, I wonder about my future. I'm interested in a job at the bank, but can I really do this with my English? I will graduate soon, so I have to be ready. Yes, I'm a student, but my life is not as easy as people think.

_____

_____

_____

_____

_____

_____

_____

(continued)

_____

_____

_____

_____

_____

_____

■ CHAPTER QUIZ

Exercise 22 **Part 1: Synthesis.** Circle the letter of the correct answer.

1. When Sammy started his studies _____ Rice University, he chose biology as his college major.

    A. at   C. by

    B. in   D. on

2. Can you explain his question _____ the subject?

    A. of   C. by

    B. about   D. in

3. My professor comes to school _____ bike. I see her pedaling down the street every day.

    A. at   C. by

    B. in   D. on

4. Winters _____ Washington, D.C., are not so cold. In fact, it does not snow very often.

    A. at   C. by

    B. in   D. on

5. _____ the Civil War, thousands of soldiers were killed.

    A. At   C. By

    B. In   D. On

6. What time did your plane land _____ Miami International Airport?

    A. at   C. by

    B. in   D. on

Part 2: Error Correction. One of the four underlined words or phrases is not correct. Circle the letter of the error and correct it in the space provided.

7. In the U.S. the state with the most people is California. Other U.S. states with large
       A   **B**   **C**

   populations include New York and Pennsylvania in the Northeast.
                                                D

   _____

8. Marie Curie was exceptional child. She was able to read fluently by the time she
                 A   **B**

   was four years old and amazed her family with her incredible memory.
         C   **D**

   _____

9. Unfortunately, Larry not come to class yesterday because he had a cold. I think he
                        A   **B**   **C**

   is feeling better today. _____
    D

10. In the age of fifteen, Marie began studying chemistry and physics at the Sorbonne
     A   **B**   **C**

    University in Paris. _____
         D

■ ORIGINAL WRITING

Exercise 23   On a separate sheet of paper, write an original paragraph (eight to twelve sentences) about your future plans. Be sure to discuss what you want to do and why. What opportunities and problems can you see? Give specific examples. In your paragraph, use at least eight of the nouns, verbs, or adjectives and their prepositions from this chapter. Underline these words.

Adjectives

Adjectives describe. As you learned in Chapter 1, they describe nouns and pronouns. In this chapter, you will review different types of adjectives, alone and in combination with other words, and how they can improve your writing.

7.1   Placement of Adjectives

Adjectives are a very common part of speech in English. They add description and details to a topic. Adjectives can describe physical characteristics (*big, heavy, Japanese*) or explain more abstract concepts (*important, hungry, difficult*).

Adjectives generally occur in two places in the sentence. The first place is before a noun, and the second place is after the verb *be*.

Before noun:	She bought a **green** *sweater.*
After be:	The sweater *is* **green.**
Before noun:	Monica always needs a **strong** *cup* of coffee in the morning.
After be:	The coffee *was* **strong.**

Do not put an adjective after a noun. Adjectives go before nouns.

Incorrect:	She bought a *sweater* ~~green.~~
Correct:	She bought a **green** *sweater.*

Adjectives can also be used after verbs that are similar to the verb *be*, such as *feel, seem,* and *appear.* (These special verbs are called linking verbs.)

My friend does not *seem* **intelligent,** but in fact he is a genius!

Exercise 1 Read the paragraph about the desert. Underline the twelve adjectives. The first one has been done for you.

Desert Life

The desert is a <u>beautiful</u> place to visit.

From a distance, the desert may look dry and

brown, but if you look closely, the desert is

full of life! Many animals live in the desert

although it is difficult to see them. If you

look carefully, you can see tiny scorpions,

poisonous snakes, and even wild rabbits.

There are various things to explore in the

desert, from the unique plants and animals

to the sandy dunes.

Exercise 2 Read the following paragraph describing a particular house. Write any appropriate adjectives in the blanks. The first one has been done for you.

The House on the Corner

There is a _____*huge*_____ house on the corner of my street. It is
　　　　　　　　　1

_____ and white, with _____ windows and a
　　　2　　　　　　　　　　　　　　　3

_____ front door. The house sits on more than one acre of land,
　　　4

and it is surrounded by _____ bushes and _____
　　　　　　　　　　　　　　5　　　　　　　　　　　　　　6

trees. The lawn is perfectly _____, like a _____
　　　　　　　　　　　　　　　　7　　　　　　　　　　　　8

carpet. I love to walk by this _____ house!
　　　　　　　　　　　　　　　　9

Adjectives do not always occur independently in sentences. Sometimes they are paired with prepositions. (See Chapter 6 for a review of prepositions.) It is important for you to learn these *adjective + preposition* combinations.

> They are **interested in** sports.

> The thief was **guilty of** the crime.

Try to remember these *adjective + preposition* combinations because they are not interchangeable.

adjective + *of*	adjective + *for*	adjective + *about*	adjective + *to*
*ashamed **of**	famous **for**	anxious **about**	*accustomed **to**
aware **of**	responsible **for**	enthusiastic **about**	
capable **of**	sorry **for**	serious **about**	
fond **of**			
guilty **of**	adjective + *with*	adjective + *in*	
proud **of**	*pleased **with**	*interested **in**	
sick **of**	happy **with**		
*tired **of**			

All of these *adjective + preposition* combinations are followed by a noun.

> I eat hamburgers for lunch every day. I am **tired of** the same *food.*
> ADJ + PREP + NOUN

If the word after the preposition is a verb, you must use the *-ing* form of the verb. (This *-ing* form of the verb is actually a noun and is called a gerund. Gerunds always end in *-ing*.)

> I eat hamburgers for lunch every day. I am **tired of** *eating* the same food.
> ADJ + PREP + NOUN (gerund)

Do not use the base form of a verb after a preposition. You must use the gerund (*-ing*) form.

Incorrect:	Are you **interested in** ~~go~~ to the store with us?
Correct:	Are you **interested in** *going* to the store with us?
Incorrect:	Are you **accustomed to** ~~drive~~ this car?
Correct:	Are you **accustomed to** *driving* this car?

---

*Adjectives that end in *-ed* are called participial adjectives. You will learn more about them in Section 7.4.

Exercise 3   Read the paragraph about education. Underline the ten *adjective + preposition* combinations. Circle the nine gerunds that follow prepositions. The first two have been done for you.

Education

Most college students are <u>aware of</u> the importance of education. However, many college students are <u>famous for</u> (avoiding) academic activities at all costs. It seems that some young people are not interested in learning. After many years in school, students get a little tired of studying every day. Young adults should remain serious about completing their studies. Everyone is capable of achieving great things, but it takes a lot of hard work. Unfortunately, some young people are not always enthusiastic about working hard. Remember, students must be responsible for shaping their futures. Many people are guilty of not studying hard while in college. Don't grow up to be one of those people who is ashamed of wasting his or her college days. Use this important time wisely. There is plenty of time to relax later.

Exercise 4 Complete each sentence by writing an adjective in the space provided. Refer to the list of *adjective + preposition* combinations on p. 139. Hint: Study the preposition in the sentence to help you choose an appropriate adjective. The first one has been done for you.

1. I am _____proud_____ of getting an A+ on the final exam! I studied very hard for it.

2. I am _____ for making cookies. Everyone in my hometown knows about my excellent cookie recipes.

3. I am _____ about going to the dentist tomorrow. I am afraid that my dentist will find more cavities on my teeth.

4. I am _____ in seeing the new horror movie this weekend. In fact, I have a collection of scary movies on DVD.

5. I am very _____ of eating the food in the cafeteria! The cooks *always* cook the same food!

6. I am _____ to going to school early. I don't need an alarm clock because I wake up at 5:30 every day.

7. I am _____ about going on a diet. My clothes don't fit me anymore. It's time to lose weight.

8. I am _____ of leaving the door unlocked.

7.3	*Be* + Adjective Combinations

One common sentence pattern in English is with the verb *be* + adjective. (See Chapter 8 for more information.)

    Josh *is* **afraid** of spiders.
       BE   ADJ

Some *be* + adjective combinations can be followed by infinitives. Remember: an infinitive form is the word *to* + the base form of the verb. Every verb has an infinitive form. *To swim, to eat, to live,* and *to be* are all examples of the infinitive.

    Evelyn *is* **afraid** <u>to touch</u> spiders.
       BE   ADJ INFINITIVE

Here is a list of adjectives that are commonly followed by an infinitive.

afraid	*disappointed	happy	*scared
*amazed	eager	lucky	sorry
angry	*encouraged	*pleased	upset
anxious	*excited	*prepared	willing
*astonished	*fascinated	proud	
careful	fortunate	ready	
curious	*frightened	reluctant	
*determined	glad	sad	

Exercise 5   Rewrite the following sentence parts about camping in correct sentence order. Circle the *be* + adjective + infinitive combinations. Hint: Look for the capitalized word to start your sentence. Look for end punctuation to finish it. The first one has been done for you.

1. an invitation to go camping / I was pleased to accept / with some friends from work.

   I (was pleased to accept) an invitation to go camping with some friends from work.

2. I was / anything about camping. / to go, but I didn't know / curious

   _____

   _____

---

*These adjectives are called participial adjectives. They are formed by adding *-ed* or *-ing* to a verb. You will learn more about them in Section 7.4.

We *were* **excited** to hear the news!

Felix *was* **ready** to move into a bigger apartment.

3. professional campers, / to travel with them. / Because my friends are / I was happy

_____

_____

4. that I didn't own a backpack. / to discover / My friends were surprised

_____

_____

5. during this short weekend trip. / to watch everything they did / I was careful

_____

_____

6. I was eager / Once the car was packed, / to begin the journey.

_____

_____

7. all of their camping secrets. / During the trip, / to teach me / my friends were determined

_____

_____

8. I am very proud / a great job on my first camping trip. / to say that I did

_____

_____

7.4 Participial Adjectives

Unlike other adjectives, participial adjectives come from verbs. The two forms of participial adjectives from regular verbs are:

present participle (VERB + -*ing*) exciting

past participle (VERB + -*ed*)* excited

_____

*The past participle of regular verbs ends in -*ed*: work, worked, worked. However, there are many irregular verbs: choose, chose, chosen.

The chosen candidates appeared on television.

This is how participial adjectives are used in sentences:

present participle: That **laughing** man is my cousin. (= He is laughing now.)

past participle: I do not like **burned** toast. (= Someone burned the toast.)

Hint: To identify a participle as an adjective, try substituting another adjective in its place.

That **laughing** man is my cousin.   →   **happy**   →   That **happy** man is my cousin.

I don't like **burned** toast.   →   **black**   →   I don't like **black** toast.

Uses of Participial Adjectives

1. The (present) participial adjective, with an *-ing* ending, gives information about the noun.

   Tessa got some **surprising** news when she saw the lottery numbers on television. (*Surprising* describes the type of news it was. She was not expecting the news.)

   I saw an **interesting** movie. (The movie causes interest.)

   Bill Smith's latest novel is **depressing.** (*Depressing* describes what type of book it is.)

2. The (past) participial adjective, with an *-ed* ending, describes the *receiver* of the action.

   The **surprised** lottery winner began to cry when she received her check.

   My uncle is an **interested** television viewer. (Television programs interest him.)

   I was **depressed** after I read Bill Smith's book. (The book made me feel sad.)

Exercise 6   Read the sentences about eating a better diet. Underline the participial adjectives. The first one has been done for you.

1. Recent statistics on obesity and poor health are

   frightening.

2. Most people are interested in maintaining a healthy

   lifestyle, but changing eating habits is never easy.

3. Healthy food does not necessarily mean boring

   food.

4. Many people decide to change their lifestyles

   because of some embarrassing situation they had.

5. People can do many things to stay in shape.

   They can join a gym, buy new aerobics shoes,

   and, most important, eliminate fattening food

   from their diet.

6. Most people start a new diet with amazing enthusiasm, but it is very difficult to stay in this new routine.

7. Having a healthy body is a very motivating factor for many people.

8. With so many different diets available today, some dieters are confused.

9. It is important to consult a doctor or nutritionist. You can feel relaxed because you are in the hands of a professional who will guide you through this challenging experience.

10. It is very exciting to know that after only a few weeks of dieting and exercise, a person can see significant improvements physically.

Exercise 7 Read the paragraph about the difficulties involved in moving. Circle the correct form of the word in parentheses. The first one has been done for you.

Moving

Moving into a new house or apartment can be (excited / (exciting)) as well as
1

(tired / tiring). Many people become (frightened / frightening) at the idea of putting
2 **3**

all of their worldly possessions into boxes and moving them to the other side of the

world—or even the other side of town. It's important to look for a new home in an

(interested / interesting) area of town. You will be more (motivated / motivating) to
4 **5**

get moved into the new place quickly. Try to sell or throw away anything that you

don't absolutely need. It's bad luck to fill up your new home with old junk. You will

be (surprised / surprising) by all the useless items that can be eliminated during the
6

moving process.

7.5 Adjective Clauses

As we have seen, adjectives may take the form of single words or phrases. Another way to add details to a sentence is to use an adjective clause. (See more about adjective clauses in Chapter 9.)

A simple adjective clause has a relative pronoun (that, which, who, whom) followed by a verb and sometimes an object. An adjective clause describes the noun(s) that comes before it.

ADJ CLAUSE

Minestrone is a thick soup   that   contains   vegetables.

NOUN   REL PRONOUN   VERB   OBJ

This sentence was formed from two sentences:

(1) Minestrone is a *thick soup*. (2) The *soup* contains vegetables.

Notice how the information "soup" is found in both sentences.

To form adjective clauses, the repeated information is replaced by a relative pronoun. If the information is a thing, we use *which* or *that*.

(1) *The girl* is my best friend. (2) *The girl* lives next door.

In these sentences, the repeated information is "girl." To form the adjective clause, we use the relative pronoun *who* and embed the second sentence into the first.

ADJ CLAUSE

The girl **who lives next door** is my best friend.

Remember to use *that* or *which* for things. (*That* is more common.) Use *who* or *that* for people. (*Who* is preferred.)

Exercise 8   Match two sentence parts to form complete sentences. The first one has been done for you.

Professions

_c_ 1. Marketing is a field

a. who assist passengers on an airplane.

_____ 2. Doctors are professionals

b. that produces high-tech, hand-held equipment.

_____ 3. Translators are people

c. that deals with selling products.

_____ 4. Microtechnology is the field

d. that examines important dates, people, and cultural events of the past.

_____ 5. Interior design is a career

e. who studies animals.

_____ 6. A zoologist is a person

f. who need to know two languages very well.

_____ 7. Flight attendants are people

g. that requires knowledge of decoration and color combinations.

_____ 8. History is a field of study

h. who care for sick people.

Exercise 9 The following vocabulary words are items commonly found in a drugstore. Choose five of the words or phrases in the box and write a short definition for each, using an adjective clause. Circle the adjective clauses. The first one has been done for you.

| fashion magazine | aspirin | paperback novel | lipstick |
| chewing gum | candy bars | laundry detergent | pencils |

1. Aspirin is a medicine (that helps reduce headaches.)

2. _____

3. _____

4. _____

5. _____

6. _____

Exercise 10 Read the paragraph about an exotic fruit. Look for nine errors in adjective placement, prepositions, gerunds, participial adjectives, infinitives, and relative pronouns. Find and correct the errors. Hint: The numbers in the left margin tell you how many errors are in each line.

A Strange South American Fruit

1   I am a person which is fond of both cooking and eating. I thought I knew

everything about food, but this was not true. I am also the kind of person who is

2   interested in try new foods and dishes ethnic, so I travel a lot in search of exotic

cuisine. During one of my culinary adventures through South America, I was

1   amazing to discover something that I had never heard of. I was completely

astonished to find something so delicious! What was this new food? It is a fruit

called the cherimoya, and it is absolutely delicious. The best way to describe

(continued)

a cherimoya is to say that it is a combination of an apple and a honeydew melon.

A ripe cherimoya is a lumpy fruit that is the size of a small melon. It has a soft green

2 skin who is fuzzy to the touch. I am not afraid for try new things, so when I saw

1 one in the market, I wanted to taste it. It is surprising that such a fruit ugly can be

so delicious. The fruit seller was happy to see my reaction. The inside of the fruit is

soft and white, and it has dark seeds. The flavor is difficult to describe, but I can say

that I will never get tired of it. The cherimoya is soft and sweet. I was delighted to

discover such a rare and delicious new fruit but sad that I could not bring one back

2 with me. I had to leave my excited new fruit what I found in South America, but

I will always have my memories (and pictures) of the cherimoya.

GUIDED WRITING

Exercise 11   Read the paragraph below. Rewrite it by making the eleven changes listed here. Careful: You may have to make other changes.

1. Omit the phrase *in college.*

2. Change *Jan Schwartz* to *David Schwartz.*

3. Replace the adjective *engaging* in sentence three with another adjective.

4. Combine sentences two and three with a coordinating conjunction (*for, and, nor, but, or, yet, so*).

5. Add an adjective clause that tells the following information about the chapters: *The chapters are in our textbook.*

6. Add an adjective clause that tells the following information about the comprehension questions: *The questions are at the end of each chapter.*

7. Change the time of the quizzes from *every week* to *every other week.*

8. Change the phrase *but the quizzes* to *but these quizzes.*

9. Remove all contractions.

10. In the last sentence, add an adjective to describe this professor.

11. Add a final sentence to the paragraph using the future tense.

My Favorite Class

    My sociology class in college is my favorite class. Professor Jan Schwartz teaches the class. Her lectures are engaging. She is knowledgeable about the subject matter, and she is more than happy to help us if we have questions. The reading for the class is interesting. The chapters are easy to read, and the comprehension questions are varied. Professor Schwartz gives us a quiz every week, but the quizzes aren't difficult if we read the material. I truly enjoy this class, and I hope to take another class with this professor next semester.

_____

_____

_____

_____

_____

_____

_____

_____

_____

_____

_____

_____

_____

Exercise 12   **Part 1: Synthesis.** Circle the letter of the correct answer.

1. Everyone thinks that that _____ is mine, but it belongs to my sister.

   A. car old green

   B. old green car

   C. green car old

   D. old greens car

2. Melissa's parents were very proud _____ her. She graduated from college with honors.

   A. in

   B. for

   C. about

   D. of

3. Nobody from my class was interested _____ to the park. They said the weather was too cold.

   A. in to go

   B. in going

   C. in go

   D. by going

4. Is everyone ready _____? It's late, and I want to get home before it gets dark!

   A. to leave

   B. for leaving

   C. leave

   D. for to leave

5. Lorraine got some _____ news yesterday.

   A. surprised very

   B. very surprised

   C. very surprising

   D. surprising very

6. Opera is a style of music _____ in Italy.

   A. who beginning

   B. began

   C. that beginning

   D. that began

Part 2: Error Correction. One of the four underlined words or phrases is not correct. Circle the letter of the error and correct it in the space provided.

7. That <u>screaming</u> baby <u>are giving</u> me a headache. I <u>want</u> to <u>change</u> our seats before the
         A   **B**   **C**   **D**
   plane takes off. _____

8. <u>Aren't</u> you tired <u>in</u> <u>waiting</u> for spring? Why <u>don't</u> we move to California where the
     A   **B** **C**   **D**
   weather is perfect all year round? _____

9. No one <u>in class</u> <u>is</u> used to <u>take</u> a quiz every week. <u>It's just</u> too much work.
          A   B   C   D

_____

10. Have you seen the <u>interesting sculpture</u> in the park? I heard that it <u>was created</u> by a
                                  A   B

<u>sculptor famous</u> <u>who</u> came from France. _____
        C   D

■ ORIGINAL WRITING

Exercise 13   On a separate sheet of paper, write a paragraph (five to eight sentences) about your favorite food. Begin by defining the food. (Use an adjective clause in the definition. Example: *Lasagna is a pasta dish that is made with several layers of lasagna noodles.*) Include any particular memory you have about this food. For example, can you recall when you first ate this food? (*The first time that I ate XYZ was when . . .*) Use participial adjectives and adjective + preposition combinations. Underline all the adjectives in your paragraph. Circle the participial adjectives and put two lines under the adjective + preposition combinations that you studied in this chapter.

Sentence Patterns with Verbs, Adjectives, and Adverbs

You learned in Chapter 1 that each word in a sentence has a specific function, or part of speech. In this chapter, you will practice different sentence patterns with these parts of speech.

8.1 Sentences with *be*

The verb *be* is the most commonly used verb in the English language. Study the following sentence patterns that use the verb *be*.

8.1.1 Subject + *be* + Complement (noun)

In this sentence pattern, the subject (before the verb) and the complement (after the verb) are the same thing. The verb *be* is like an equal (=) sign between them.

My mother is a teacher at our local middle school.
 SUBJ BE COMPLEMENT
 mother = teacher

Mr. Jones was the bank president for twenty years.
 SUBJ BE COMPLEMENT
 Mr. Jones = president

Paris is the capital of France.
 SUBJ BE COMPLEMENT
 Paris = capital

The reason that we selected this hotel for the meeting is the price of the room.
        SUBJ   BE COMPLEMENT
        reason   = price

Match the two sentence parts to form complete sentences. The first one has been done for you.

__f__	1. Literature class is	a.	my favorite sport.
_____	2. I am	b.	my good friends.
_____	3. California is	c.	a talented pianist.
_____	4. My classmates are	d.	college sweethearts.
_____	5. My mother and father were	e.	the state where I live.
_____	6. Soccer is	f.	my first class in the morning.

Exercise 2 Using the sentences in Exercise 1 as examples, complete the following sentences, adding a form of the verb *be* and a complement. The first one has been done for you.

1. A Ferrari _is a fast sports car._____

2. Karate _____

3. Angelina Jolie _____

4. My oldest aunt _____

5. The Coliseum in Rome _____

6. The tallest person in my class _____

7. McDonald's _____

8. William Shakespeare _____

9. *The Titanic* _____

10. Princess Diana _____

8.1.2 Subject + be + Adjective

An adjective after the verb *be* is a common sentence pattern. The adjective describes the subject.

The children were **hungry** after their field trip to the state park.
   SUBJ   BE   ADJ

Our company's **software engineers** are very **talented**.
                SUBJ   BE   ADJ

Linda's **hairstyle is unique**.
    SUBJ BE ADJ

Exercise 3 Read the paragraph about food poisoning. Underline the subjects and circle their corresponding adjectives. There are six. The first one has been done for you.

Food Sickness

I was very (ill) yesterday. I went to a restaurant with some friends the other night, and we all had fish. When I woke up yesterday, I was sweaty and had a fever. I called my friends, and they were sick, too. I could not eat anything! My brother was worried about me, so he called our family doctor. The doctor told him that I had food poisoning. He also said that it usually lasts between twenty-four and forty-eight hours. My brother made me some tea and dry toast and forced me to eat. I was dehydrated, so I had to drink plenty of water. Today I am better, but I did not go to work. I cannot believe that I suffered so much just from eating a piece of fish!

Exercise 4 Choose a famous person, such as an actor, a politician, or an athlete. Write five sentences about that person, using adjectives to describe him or her. Use the *be* + adjective pattern in your sentences. Circle the adjectives you use.

Famous Person: _____

1. _____

2. _____

3. _____

4. _____

5. _____

8.1.3   *Subject + be + Prepositional Phrase*

We often add a prepositional phrase to a sentence when the verb *be* is the main verb. This type of sentence generally answers the question *where?*

The library books are on the shelf.
　　　SUBJ　　　　　BE　　prep phrase

Tammy is in the park today.
　SUBJ　BE　PREP PHRASE

The city of Key West is near Cuba.
　　　　SUBJ　　　　　　BE prep phrase

Exercise 5   Read the paragraph. Underline all of the *be* verb + prepositional phrase combinations. There are five. The first one has been done for you.

> ## Wedding
>
> My best friend Magda is getting married next week. She <u>is from Hungary</u>, and I have known her for five years. She and her boyfriend met in college. They were in the same freshman English class. Magda and Mike also lived in the same apartment complex, so they saw each other all the time. They asked me to be the maid of honor, so I will be in the wedding. Both Magda and Mike are so excited about next week! I am, too. They have spent a lot of time and money to prepare for the wedding. Yesterday the three of us were in my driveway, talking about all of their good and bad times. It is hard to believe that next weekend they will be on their honeymoon.

Exercise 6   Choose six phrases from the box as subjects and write sentences using the verb *be* + prepositional phrases. The first one has been done for you.

My backpack	~~The teacher~~	The blackboard	My friend
The light switch	My textbook	My pen	My classroom

1. The teacher is in the front of the classroom.

2. _____

3. _____

4. _____

5. _____

6. _____

8.1.4   *Subject + be + Present Participle (verb + -ing)*

In this sentence pattern, you combine the verb *be* with a present participle to form the progressive tense. (See Chapter 2 for more information on the present progressive and past progressive tenses.)

<u>The students</u> <u>are studying</u> for the final exam right now. (present progressive)
   SUBJ   BE + present participle

<u>The members</u> of the United Nations <u>were discussing</u> a trade embargo. (past progressive)
   SUBJ   BE + present participle

Exercise 7   Read the paragraph about a student named Michael. Change the underlined verbs to *be* + present participle. The first one has been done for you.

Mastering New Vocabulary

             is sitting
Michael <u>sits</u> in class. He <u>listens</u> to his teacher explain vocabulary. He <u>writes</u>

the information in his notebook. Michael <u>tries</u> to understand every word, but it is

difficult. Tomorrow he <u>takes</u> a test on these vocabulary words. In fact, he and his

classmates <u>meet</u> after class for a study session. Michael <u>improves</u> his vocabulary

day by day.

Exercise 8   Read the paragraph about the city of Florence, Italy. Complete the sentences with appropriate words using the forms indicated in parentheses. The first one has been done for you.

Florence

Florence, Italy, ——————— *is a popular city* ———————

                    1

(*be* + complement). Florence is in the Tuscany region, which is the northwestern

part of Italy. Florence ————————————————————————————

                              2

(*be* + adjective) because it has so many museums and parks to visit. The famous

Uffizi Museum is in the center of town. Within walking distance of the museum,

tourists can see the most famous of Michelangelo's sculptures, the David. David

———————————————————— (*be* + adjective) because of his

        3

(continued)

anatomical features. Another interesting place to visit is the Ponte Vecchio, or

Old Bridge. The Ponte Vecchio _____
                                              4

(*be* + prepositional phrase), so tourists can easily walk there from the main

train station. Thousands of people walk over the bridge every day. The bridge

_____ (*be* + complement) and contains
                5

many small shops where people can buy jewelry. All in all, the attractions in

Florence _____ (*be* + adjective), historic,
                          6

and memorable.

8.2 Sentence Patterns with Transitive and Intransitive Verbs

8.2.1 *Subject + Verb + Object (transitive verbs)*

One of the most basic sentence patterns in English is Subject + Verb + Object (S + V + O)

Subject	Verb	Object
Kenny	likes	pizza.
Lisa	is taking	the medicine.
The child	caught	the firefly.

In all of the above examples, the verb must have a direct object that answers the question "What?" or "Who?" Verbs that need objects are called **transitive verbs.**

Kenny likes what? Kenny likes **pizza.**

Lisa is taking what? Lisa is taking **the medicine.**

The child caught what? The child caught **the firefly.**

If you write a sentence using a transitive verb and leave out the object, the sentence is wrong. It is unfinished and does not make sense.

Incorrect: ~~Kenny likes~~. (What does Kenny like? Who does Kenny like?)

Incorrect: ~~Lisa is taking~~. (What is Lisa taking?)

Incorrect: ~~The child caught~~. (What did the child catch?)

Exercise 9 Read the sentences. Underline the subject and put two lines under the verb. Then write an appropriate object in the blank. The first one has been done for you.

1. At my school, <u>students</u> <u><u>use</u></u> _____*reference books*_____ to help them study better.

2. Before going to work, Cathy wrote _____ .

3. I study _____ whenever I have some free time.

4. According to my professor, college students should read _____

   every day.

5. I changed my _____ because the information was too difficult.

6. The teacher gave _____ this morning.

7. I cannot check out books from the library. I don't have _____ .

8. Over the weekend, Professor Smith finally corrected _____ .

8.2.2   *Subject + Verb (intransitive verbs)*

Intransitive verbs have the pattern S + V and do *not* take a direct object.

<u>**Lisa**</u> <u><u>**complained**</u></u>.
SUBJ   VERB

<u>**We**</u> <u><u>**fell**</u></u> into the pool.
SUBJ VERB (prepositional phrase)

<u>**I**</u> <u><u>**am working**</u></u> diligently.
SUBJ   VERB   (adverb of manner)

Notice that if there is additional information after the main verb, it is *not* a direct object.

Some verbs are always transitive, some verbs are always intransitive, and some verbs can be transitive or intransitive. Your dictionary probably marks verbs as *vt*, *vi*, or *v* to indicate these three possibilities.

transitive: <u>**Gerry**</u> <u><u>**eats**</u></u> <u>**hamburgers**</u>.
            SUBJ   VERB   OBJ

intransitive: <u>**Gerry**</u> <u><u>**eats**</u></u> in the cafeteria.
            SUBJ   VERB (prepositional phrase)

transitive: **The students are studying Latin.**
                   SUBJ   VERB   OBJ

intransitive: **The students are studying.**
                   SUBJ   VERB

Exercise 10   Read the sentences about sports utility vehicles, which are commonly referred to as SUVs. If the sentence has a direct object, circle the object.

1. Sports utility vehicles (SUVs) cost a lot of (money).

2. They are very popular, however.

3. Five SUVs are in the parking lot right now.

4. SUVs use lots of gasoline.

5. Carolyn doesn't have enough money to buy an SUV.

6. Hummer makes three types of SUVs.

7. We are taking our SUV on vacation next month.

8. Have you ever driven an SUV?

Exercise 11   Write seven sentences about your typical day, beginning with when you wake up. Try to use at least one example of each of the following: *be* + complement, *be* + adjective, *be* + prepositional phrase, transitive verb, intransitive verb.

1. _____

2. _____

3. _____

4. _____

5. _____

6. _____

7. _____

8.3   Sentence Patterns with Adverbs

It is important to know where to place adverbs in sentences. Different types of adverbs are placed in different places.

8.3.1   *Adverbs of Manner*

As you know from Chapter 1, **adverbs** modify verbs. **Adverbs of manner** give extra information about the verb. They help describe how an action takes place.

> Sherry sang the song **beautifully.** (explains how Sherry sang)
>
> The newscaster speaks **clearly.** (explains how the newscaster speaks)
>
> I finished the test **quickly.** (explains how I finished the test)

Note that most adverbs of manner are formed by adding the suffix *-ly* to an adjective. Three common adverbs of manner that do not have the *-ly* ending are:

> *well:*   The athletes ran the marathon **well.**
>
> *fast:*   My French teacher talks too **fast.**
>
> *hard:*   You have to study **hard** in chemistry class if you want to pass the final exam.

Placement of Adverbs of Manner

With transitive verbs (verbs that take an object), adverbs of manner are generally placed after the direct object.

> Sherry sang the song **beautifully.**
>   OBJ   ADV

With intransitive verbs (verbs that do not take an object), adverbs of manner can come after the verb or after a prepositional phrase.

> The president speaks **clearly** to the press.
>   VERB   ADV   (prepositional phrase)

> The president speaks to the press **clearly.**
>   VERB   prep phrase   ADV

Exercise 12   Read the sentences about a person who is very interested in astronomy. If the placement of the adverb of manner is correct, write C on the line. If the placement is not correct, write X and make the necessary changes. The first one has been done for you.

_____X_____ 1. Joann does her astronomy ~~quickly~~

　　　　　　　　　　　　quickly
homework every day.
　　　　　　　　　　　　　^

_____ 2. Her new telescope works well.

_____ 3. With a telescope, she can see clearly the

stars.

_____ 4. Joann notices intently the constellations.

_____ 5. During the full moon, Joann watches incessantly the sky.

_____ 6. Joann's astronomy instructor speaks very softly.

8.3.2   *Adverbs of Place and Time*

Adverbs of place tell *where* something happened. Two common adverbs of place are *here* and *there*.

> Marcia left her house key **here**. (explains where Marcia left the key)

> I parked my car **there**. (explains where the car is parked)

Adverbs of time tell *when* something happened. Some common adverbs of time are *soon, yesterday, tomorrow, next week,* and *then*.

> My favorite TV show starts **soon**. (explains when the show starts)

> The race will be held **next week**. (explains when the race will be held)

When you use both an adverb of time and an adverb of place in a sentence, be sure to put the adverb of place before the adverb of time. An easy way to remember this is that the letter P (place) comes before the letter T (time) in the alphabet.

Incorrect:　　I need to be ~~tomorrow in Miami~~.

Correct:　　　I need to be in Miami tomorrow.

Exercise 13   Rearrange the following sentence parts in the correct order. Hint: Look for the capitalized word to start your sentence. The first one has been done for you.

1. are flying to Washington, D.C. / Kelly and I / tomorrow afternoon

   Kelly and I are flying to Washington, D.C. tomorrow afternoon.
   _____

2. quickly / yesterday / changed / The weather in Washington

   _____

3. next year / will occur / The presidential elections

   _____

4. starts / in five minutes / The presidential debate

   _____

5. more than forty years ago / President Kennedy / died

   _____

6. are meeting us / Leslie and Donna / in Washington / this weekend

   _____

8.3.3   *Adverbs of Frequency*

Adverbs of frequency tell *how often* something happens. Some common adverbs of frequency are listed below.

always------------100% of the time

usually

often

sometimes------ 50% of the time

rarely

seldom

never-------------0% of the time

Friday is **always** "casual day" at my company. (explains how often casual day happens)

I **seldom** wear a tie on "casual day." (explains how often I wear a tie)

Placement of Adverbs of Frequency

Adverbs of frequency can occur in different positions in a sentence. They can occur after the verb *be* or after *modals* (*can, could,* etc.).

He *is* **always** late to class.

They can occur before any other verb.

Karen **never** *eats* meat.

note: The most usual place for adverbs of frequency is within the sentence as explained already. However, adverbs of frequency can occur at the beginning or end of a sentence. (Exception: *Always* cannot begin a sentence.)

Usual position: middle:	All parents **sometimes** get angry with their children.
Beginning:	**Sometimes** all parents get angry with their children.
End:	All parents get angry with their children **sometimes.**

Exercise 14   Read each activity and write a sentence explaining *how often* you do this activity. Use the adverbs of frequency from Section 8.3.3. Circle the adverb you use in each sentence. The first one has been done for you.

1. eat in a restaurant   I (rarely) eat in a restaurant. _____

2. study vocabulary   _____

3. go to the movies   _____

4. call my family   _____

5. order Chinese food   _____

6. listen to hip-hop music   _____

7. read e-mail   _____

8. ride a motorcycle   _____

9. write to a celebrity   _____

10. play outdoor sports   _____

Exercise 15 Read the paragraph below. Rewrite it by making the nine changes listed. Careful: You may have to make other changes.

1. In the first sentence, change *a fitness club* to *fitness clubs.*

2. In the second sentence, the verb *has* is correct, but good writing needs more variety of vocabulary. Change *has* to the synonyms *features* or *offers.*

3. Add the adjective *extensive* to describe the word *variety.*

4. Replace the adjectives *simple* and *useful* with two other adjectives.

5. Combine sentences five and six.

6. Add the adverb *often* to your new sentence.

7. Add the adverb *sometimes* to the sentence that talks about special classes.

8. Replace *a good idea* with another complement.

9. Add a sentence with the subject *fitness clubs*, the verb *be*, and a prepositional phrase as the final sentence in the paragraph.

Fitness Clubs

A fitness club is a wonderful place to get in shape. First of all, every good fitness club has a variety of types of machines and equipment. A member can go into any fitness club and exercise for hours without using the same piece of equipment. The equipment is

simple and useful. Fitness clubs have swimming pools. Fitness clubs have spas. For even more practice, special classes are available. They include yoga and basic martial arts. All in all, exercising in a fitness club is a good idea.

_____

_____

_____

_____

_____

_____

(continued)

■ CHAPTER QUIZ

Exercise 16   **Part 1: Synthesis.** Circle the letter of the correct answer.

1. My sister loves her computer. In fact, she _____ every day.

   A. use it   C. uses

   B. uses it   D. use

2. Carlos is an excellent chef. He _____ an Italian restaurant.

   A. works   C. works in

   B. work in   D. is work

3. Everyone _____ for the test, so no one should fail tomorrow.

   A. studied hard   C. hard is studying

   B. hard studied   D. is hard studying

4. Next week, _____ .

   A. on a trip we're going   C. we go on a trip

   B. on a trip we go   D. we're going on a trip

5. Although she lives just 50 miles away, Joann _____ her mother in Washington state.

   A. rarely visits   C. visits rarely

   B. visits always   D. always visits

6. Do you need _____?

   A. to go to work tomorrow   C. tomorrow to go to work

   B. to go tomorrow to work   D. go tomorrow to work

Part 2: Error Correction. One of the four underlined words or phrases is not correct. Circle the letter of the error and correct it in the space provided.

7. Leslie <u>is so</u> happy to have <u>a job new</u>. She talks <u>about</u> her wonderful new <u>boss every day</u>.
        A   B   C   D

       _____

8. My best friend <u>was for five years the school president</u>, but now <u>she is</u> in college and
                A   B   C
<u>does not</u> have time for extra activities. _____
  D

9. John and his family <u>recently moved</u> to Arizona from Maine. It <u>was</u> <u>very cold</u> in Maine.
                        A   B   C
John <u>hated</u>. _____
    D

10. I <u>cannot find</u> my reading glasses. <u>Were next to</u> my textbooks, but I <u>do not see</u> them
    A   B   C
anymore. <u>Did you</u> accidentally pick them up?
       D

       _____

■ ORIGINAL WRITING

Exercise 17   On a separate sheet of paper, write an original paragraph (eight to twelve sentences) about a typical weekend day in your life. Discuss the day from beginning to end. Be sure to include a variety of sentence patterns from this chapter with verbs, adverbs, and adjectives. Write VT above transitive verbs and VI above intransitive verbs. Check the correctness of your paragraph with a partner.

Sentence Types

In Chapter 8, you learned how different parts of a sentence come together into different patterns. In this chapter, you will work on different types of sentences. Two common sentence types are simple sentences and compound sentences.

9.1 Simple Sentence Review

All sentences must have a subject and a verb. A simple sentence consists of one subject-verb combination. However, a **simple sentence** can have more than one subject or more than one verb. Study these examples of simple sentences:

1 subject: **Paul** <u>went</u> to the mountains last weekend.

2 subjects: **Paul** and **his brother** <u>went</u> to the mountains last weekend.

3 subjects: **Paul**, **Anthony**, and **Joe** <u>went</u> to the mountains last weekend.

1 verb: The <u>secretary</u> **answered** the phone.

2 verbs: The <u>secretary</u> **answered** the phone and **wrote** a message.

3 verbs: The <u>secretary</u> **answered** the phone, **wrote** a message, and **gave** it to Mary.

Notice that the connecting word in sentences 2 and 3 is the conjunction *and*.

Exercise 1 Read these simple sentences about two family holidays. Underline the subjects once and the verbs twice. The first one has been done for you.

1. <u>Mother's Day</u> and <u>Father's Day</u> <u><u>are</u></u> popular holidays in the United States.

2. These holidays celebrate the love and hard work of our parents.

3. Popular Mother's Day gifts include flowers and jewelry.

4. Boys and girls often think up and make homemade presents for their parents.

5. I recently looked for and bought a tie for my father.

6. Some countries celebrate Children's Day and even Grandparents' Day.

7. Parents and children enjoy these holidays together.

8. Do you celebrate Mother's Day?

Exercise 2 Read the sentences about my grandparents. Add the second piece of information in parentheses (either a subject or a verb) to the original sentence to form a longer sentence. The first one has been done for you.

1. My grandmother loves to talk about the "good old days." (add subject: grandfather)

   My grandmother and grandfather love to talk about the "good old days."

2. However, they love modern inventions, especially their computer. (add verb: use)

   _____

3. My grandmother washes her new car every Saturday morning. (add verb: wax)

   _____

4. My grandmother surfs the Internet. (add subject: grandfather)

   _____

5. The e-mails come mostly from my grandmother. (add subject: instant messages)

   _____

6. My grandparents have improved our communication through the use of the Internet. (add subject: I)

   _____

7. My grandparents now trust the power of modern technology. (add verb: love)

   _____

9.2 Compound Sentences

A **compound sentence** is formed by combining two simple sentences. These two parts are joined by a (coordinating) conjunction. There are seven coordinating conjunctions in English: *for, and, nor, but, or, yet, so.* An easy way to remember the coordinating conjunctions is the mnemonic* device FANBOYS:

| F = for | A = and | N = nor | B = but | O = or | Y = yet | S = so |

The most common of these conjunctions are ***and, but, so,*** and ***or.*** (We do not use *for, nor,* and *yet* as conjunctions as often.)

and: to show additional information

> Judy loves to surf, **and** she goes to the beach every weekend.

but: to show contrast

> I am sleepy, **but** I still need to study.

so: to show a result

> My car broke down, **so** I took it to my mechanic.

or: to show options

> We can go see a movie, **or** we can rent one from the video store.

Note that a comma comes before the coordinating conjunction.

Here are examples of combining two simple sentences to form a compound sentence.

Simple sentence 1:	Sam's birthday party is next week.
Simple sentence 2:	I have invited 20 people to the party.
Compound sentence:	**Sam's birthday party is next week,** *and* **I have invited 20 people to the party.**

Simple sentence 1:	It rained very hard last night.
Simple sentence 2:	We decided to cancel our travel plans.
Compound sentence:	**It rained very hard last night,** *so* **we decided to cancel our travel plans.**

The word *so* has three meanings in English. Only one of them is a coordinating conjunction that means *result.* Only use a comma with the word *so* when it is a conjunction that means *result.*

1. I studied all night, so I am really tired today. (= result; comma is necessary)

2. I studied all night so I would pass today's test. (= purpose; never use a comma)

   I studied all night so that I would pass today's test. (*so* is a short form of *so that*)

3. I am so tired. (= very; never use a comma)

---

*Mnemonics are techniques that help you memorize important information.

Exercise 3   Read these sentence parts about transportation and pollution. Match the two sentence parts to form a compound sentence. Circle the coordinating conjunction in each sentence. The first one has been done for you.

_____d_____ 1. Motorcycles are less polluting than cars,

a. but most people still prefer to use their own vehicles.

_____ 2. Some people use public transportation,

b. and this problem will continue to grow if our leaders do not start making changes.

_____ 3. Automobiles create an enormous amount of pollution,

c. or do you drive your own car?

d. ⟨but⟩ they are also more dangerous.

_____ 4. Public buses are available in most major cities,

e. so some people use them as often as possible.

_____ 5. Pollution is a growing problem,

f. but they are also very convenient.

_____ 6. Bicycles do not cause pollution,

g. but real solutions are not always simple.

_____ 7. Do you use public transportation,

h. and these buses are often relatively inexpensive.

_____ 8. There are many theories on how to reduce pollution,

Exercise 4   Read these sentences about the community center. In each item, add another simple sentence after the conjunction to make a compound sentence. Think about the meaning of the coordinating conjunction. The first one has been done for you.

1. The community center is located in the middle of town, and ___it is a popular meeting___

    ___place.___

2. It is a large meeting hall, but _____

    _____

3. People of all ages go there regularly, and _____

    _____

4. The community center is getting old, so _____

    _____

5. Town leaders can try to raise taxes to fix up the center, or _____

    _____

6. Everyone hopes that the center will stay around forever, but _____

    _____

9.3   Better Sentences with Adjective Clauses*

As you learned in Chapter 7, adjective clauses describe nouns in a sentence. Adjective clauses cannot stand alone as a sentence, and they are usually introduced by the relative pronouns *that, which,* or *who.* Study these examples.

My sister lives in a house ***that* is over 100 years old.**

In this example, two sentences are combined:

1. My sister lives in a house.   and

2. The house is over 100 years old.

People ***who* drive SUVs** are becoming more and more concerned with gas mileage.

In this example, two sentences are combined:

1. People are becoming more and more concerned with gas mileage.   and

2. People drive SUVs.

---

* Sentences with adjective clauses can be classified as complex sentences.

I truly enjoyed the book ***that I read over the winter holidays.*** (The adjective clause describes which book.)

In this example, two sentences are combined:

1. I truly enjoyed the <u>book</u>.   and

2. I read the <u>book</u> over the winter holidays.

Exercise 5 Read the paragraph about moving. Underline the adjective clauses. Circle the relative pronouns. The first one has been done for you.

Moving

Moving from one house to another can be difficult, so try to follow these steps. Always move the heavier items first. A bed (that) <u>contains a heavy frame</u> is easier to move at the beginning of the process. People who move on their own will probably want to get some friends or neighbors to help with the bigger furniture. Friends can help with pieces of furniture that are older and don't need special attention. After the big pieces are in your new home, try changing the placement. The new home that you have chosen doesn't have to be decorated in the same way as your old home. Label your boxes next. It is much easier to move boxes that are labeled with the contents and the name of the room. The kitchen is one of the most important rooms in the house, so unpack those boxes first. When the kitchen is finished, continue to the room that everyone uses at least twice a day—the bathroom. Remember: you don't need to unpack everything at one time. Just take out the most important items. By following these steps, you will be enjoying your new home in no time!

Exercise 6 Read these paragraphs about football. Combine the two sentences in parentheses into one sentence using an adjective clause, and write your answer on the lines after the paragraph. Always change the second sentence to the adjective clause. The first one has been done for you.

Football

Have you ever been to a professional

football game? (People get very excited. /
1

People go to football games.) A football game

generally lasts three hours. (Sometimes

there are games. / ~~The games~~ last longer.)
                    △ that

A football game is separated into four

quarters. Each quarter is 15 minutes long.

(The clock stops and starts regularly. / ~~The~~
    which/that
3

~~clock~~ is used at football games.) (This is much different from the clocks. / The clocks are
                                                                                    4
                                          who
used in soccer games.) (Fans like to eat specific things. / ~~Fans~~ go to football games.)
                                                          5 △

   Some popular foods include hot dogs, nachos, and big pretzels. (The food is

fairly expensive. / People eat this food.) (For a truly unique experience, go to a
        6

football game. / You will not forget the experience.)
        7

(continued)

1.   _People who go to football games get very excited._

2.   _____

3.   _____

4.   _____

5.   _____

6.   _____

7.   _____

Exercise 7   Read the compound sentences about a trip. Use the information in parentheses to create and insert adjective clauses in the correct places. Hint: Study the words in **bold** to help you insert the clause in the right place. The first one has been done for you.

1.   Vicki had a bad day yesterday, so she decided to visit her **friend.** (Her **friend** lives at the beach.) _Vicki had a bad day yesterday, so she decided to visit her friend who lives at_

the beach._

2.   The **road** was under construction, but it was not busy. (The **road** leads to the beach.)

_____

_____

3.   The 100-mile **trip** lasted less than two hours, and it was an easy drive. (Vicki took the

trip.) _____

_____

Vicki arrived at dinnertime, and her friend Lena was very happy to see her.

4.   The **dinner** was ready, and they immediately began to eat. (Lena made the **dinner.**)

_____

_____

5.   After dinner, Vicki and Lena took a long walk on the beach, and they talked about

things. (The **things** made them stressed.) _____

_____

6. Lena offered to take Vicki to a movie, or they could go to a **nightclub.** (The **nightclub** opened recently.) _____

_____

Vicki and Lena decided to stay home, but they talked for hours and hours.

7. This **trip** was very relaxing for Vicki, and she hopes to visit Lena again soon. (The **trip** was planned at the last minute.) _____

_____

9.4 Better Sentences with Adverb Clauses*

Another way to improve a sentence is to add an adverb clause. **Adverb clauses** are similar to adverbs. They help describe or modify the verb or the entire sentence. Adverb clauses have the pattern subordinating conjunction + subject + verb. Sentences with adverb clauses are classified as complex sentences. Adverb clauses are always introduced by subordinating conjunctions.

Study the examples below.

Before	I	moved	to California,	I lived in New York City.
SUBORD CONJ	SUBJ	VERB	(prep. phrase)	MAIN SENTENCE

I went to sleep early	*since*	I	was	so tired.
MAIN SENTENCE	SUBORD CONJ	SUBJ	VERB	(adjective)

Here is a list of common subordinating conjunctions.

Time	Reason / Cause	Contrast
after	because	although
before	since	while
when		
while		
whenever		

Adverb clauses can come before or after the main sentence. Put a comma after the adverb clause only if it begins the sentence.

Because Gheorghe missed the bus, he decided to take the subway. (comma needed)

ADVERB CLAUSE + MAIN CLAUSE

If the adverb clause comes after the main clause, no comma is needed. A common punctuation error is to put a comma before an adverb clause, especially with the conjunction *because.*

Gheorghe decided to take the subway **because he missed the bus.** (no comma)

MAIN CLAUSE + ADVERB CLAUSE

_____

* Sentences with adverb clauses can be classified as complex sentences.

Exercise 8   Read the sentences about finding a job after graduating from college. Underline the adverb clause and circle the subordinating conjunction. Refer to the list in Section 9.4 if necessary. Add commas where they are needed. The first one has been done for you.

Interviewing

1. (Whenever) <u>Irene looks for a new job</u>, she gets nervous.

2. Since Irene is a college graduate she feels confident about her background.

3. She often felt nervous and failed to make a great first impression because she lacked interviewing experience.

4. Although she scheduled many interviews she was not offered a job at first.

5. While many people in Irene's position would have ended their job search immediately Irene made the decision to get help from a personal coach.

6. Irene was also talking to friends about possible job openings in their companies while she was training.

7. After she successfully finished her interview training Irene was finally confident in her ability to interview for a job.

Exercise 9   Reread the sentences in Exercise 8. Write the subordinating conjunction used in each sentence, and then write its function. The first one has been done for you.

Subordinating Conjunction	Function
1. whenever	time
2. _____	_____
3. _____	_____
4. _____	_____
5. _____	_____
6. _____	_____
7. _____	_____

Exercise 10 Read the sentences about choosing a major in the hotel industry. Combine the two sentences in parentheses into one sentence with an adverb clause. Use the subordinating conjunction indicated to write your answer on the lines after the paragraph. Add commas where they are necessary. The first one has been done for you.

Choosing the Best Major

(Thomas wants to work in the hotel industry. / Thomas has decided to get a
1

degree in hotel management. / because) Hotel management is a growing business,

and young professionals have many opportunities. (There is a lot of competition

in this career. / Some universities offer excellent programs for students. / although)
2

After Thomas chose his major, he did some research on the available schools. (He

decided to apply to the University of Nevada, Las Vegas. / It has a popular degree
3

program. / because) The courses include introduction to hospitality management,

conference planning, speech, and economics. (Thomas begins his studies. / His
4

family will visit the city to find him a place to live. / before) (Thomas finishes

his program. / There will be lots of job opportunities for him within a large hotel
5

chain. / when)

(continued)

1. <u>Because Thomas wants to work in the hotel industry, he has decided to get a degree</u>

   <u>in hotel management.</u>

2. _____

   _____

3. _____

   _____

4. _____

   _____

5. _____

   _____

Exercise 11   Read the following sentences about painting a room. They are missing information. Add information to complete each sentence. Add a comma where necessary. The first one has been done for you.

1. Before I chose to paint my bedroom, <u>I did some research about popular colors.</u>

2. Bright yellow was not a good color because _____

   _____

3. While I was painting the room _____

   _____

4. After I finished the job _____

   _____

5. When I enter my room now _____

   _____

6. Making a comfortable environment was important since _____

   _____

Exercise 12 Read this paragraph about Halloween. Find and correct the six errors with punctuation, relative pronouns, and subordinating conjunctions. Hint: The numbers in the left margin tell you how many errors are in each line.

Halloween

Halloween is a very special holiday

for both children and adults. Children

1 | like to go trick-or-treating and adults

prefer to go to Halloween parties. In both

cases, everyone likes to dress up or wear

1 | a costume. Costumes who are popular

this year include pirates and superheroes.

Candy is another important element of

1 | Halloween. Chocolate, and fruit candy are

1 | children's favorites. In fact, some children eat their Halloween candy, until they get

1 | sick. It is important for parents to limit the amount of candy after their children eat

1 | too much. Halloween is a great holiday for kids but adults also like it!

Exercise 13 Read the paragraph below. Rewrite it by making the five changes listed. Careful! You may have to make other changes.

1. Add *Because the bedroom is such a personal environment* to the second sentence.

2. Add *kitchens* to the subject of sentence three.

3. Add *because it is considered a private space* to sentence four.

4. Combine sentences five and six using a coordinating conjunction.

5. Combine sentences seven and eight, making sentence eight an adjective clause.

Rules for Decorating

It is important to consider the function of a room before you decide to decorate it. Interior decorators say that this room reflects a person's personality more than any other room in the house. Living rooms are used by everyone, but the bedroom is decorated exclusively for the comfort and relaxation of the owner. The bedroom stays closed during social events such as parties and barbeques. Some people decorate their bedrooms with paintings and pictures. Others prefer a simple look. People appreciate their private place. People decorate their bedrooms with a few personal expressions.

_____

_____

_____

_____

_____

_____

_____

_____

_____

_____

_____

_____

_____

Exercise 14   **Part 1: Synthesis.** Circle the letter of the correct answer.

1. Next summer everybody in my family _____ the mountains.

   A. is going   C. is going to

   B. goes   D. goes to

2. _____ in the month of October.

   A. Halloween and Columbus Day.   C. Halloween and Columbus Day are

   B. Halloween and Columbus Day,   D. Halloween and Columbus Day are
                                          holidays, they are

3. We were extremely _____ continued working on our project.

   A. tired, but   C. tired. But

   B. tired, but we   D. tired. But we

4. Anna is very _____ she got a scholarship to Harvard.

   A. smart,   C. smart, so

   B. smart. And now   D. smart. And so

5. Athletes _____ every day dream of becoming professionals.

   A. which practice   C. practice

   B. are practicing   D. who practice

6. The student reviewed the chapter, researched at the _____ shared them with his
   classmates.

   A. library, took notes, and   C. library, took notes,

   B. library and took notes and   D. library, he took notes, and

Part 2. Error Correction. One of the four underlined words or phrases is not correct.
Circle the letter of the error and correct it in the space provided.

7. After I got home from class, I made myself a huge turkey sandwich who was delicious!
         A   B   C   D

   _____

8. Joann didn't make it to school on time yesterday, because her car broke down on
             A   B   C

   the highway. _____
        D

9. Because Sandra studied hard <u>every day this</u> whole semester, so no one
       A   **B**

   <u>was surprised</u> that she got a really high score on <u>the test that we</u> had yesterday.
       C   **D**

   _____

10. Dogs <u>who bark</u> all night drive me crazy! I want <u>to scream</u> every time the
          A   **B**

    <u>neighbor's puppy</u> Lucky starts his <u>barking</u>. _____
        C   **D**

■ ORIGINAL WRITING

Exercise 15   On a separate sheet of paper, write an original paragraph (seven to twelve sentences) about your favorite room. Describe this room in detail, including what the room looks like and what you like to do in the room. Be sure to include simple and compound sentences and label each. Use at least two adjective clauses. Underline the relative pronouns.

10 Common Grammar Errors

Like all writers, second language writers make errors in their writing. However, some errors are more serious than others because they can hide or change the writer's meaning. In this chapter, you will review some of the most common and serious errors that less experienced writers often make.

10.1 Be / Have

1. The verb *be* is often followed by an adjective.

   My mother **is** *amazing.*

   My cousin **was** *lucky* to win the prize.

   The verb *have* is not followed by an adjective.

Incorrect:	The information on the company website **has** *right.*
Correct:	The information on the company website **is** *right.*

2. Note that in these special expressions, the verb *be* (*am, is, are, was, were*) is followed by an adjective, not a noun:

be right	be wrong	be afraid	be lucky	be __ years old
be cold	be hot	be hungry	be thirsty	be angry
be sleepy	be correct	be incorrect	be careful	be ashamed

   Use *be* with a noun only when the subject and the noun refer to the same person or thing.

   My ***uncle is*** a good ***dentist.***
   SUBJ + BE   +   NOUN   (uncle = dentist)

3. Use ***have*** with a noun.

have a problem	have an accident	have a headache
have a toothache	have a sore back	have a blister
have a good time	have a bad time	have a hard time
have a broken leg	have a baby	have a talk

have good news   have bad news   have a fight

have a dream   have a nightmare   have an argument

have a discussion

My *uncle* **has** a nice *office.*

SUBJ + HAVE   +   NOUN   (uncle ≠ office)

Exercise 1   Read these sentences about a problem between two friends. Then complete each sentence with the correct form of *be* or *have*. Circle any adjectives that follow *be.* The first two have been done for you.

1. Yesterday I _____ had _____ a problem with my best friend Greta.

2. I _____ was _____ very (tired), and I _____ was _____ (sleepy).

3. She _____ some bad news about her pet dog. The day before yesterday her

    dog died.

4. Her dog _____ 12 years old.

5. Obviously, Greta _____ really sad.

6. She tried to talk to me, but I _____ very sleepy. In fact, I fell asleep twice in

    our conversation.

7. Each time I woke up right away, but of course she _____ angry.

8. I apologized at once. It _____ my mistake. I _____ completely

    wrong.

9. Greta _____ a great friend. In fact, she _____ my best friend.

10. I _____ lucky to have her as my good friend.

11. Greta and I usually _____ a good time when we see each other, but

    yesterday's meeting _____ not good.

12. Yesterday's problem _____ completely my fault. I _____ so sorry

    about falling asleep during her story.

Exercise 2   Read these sentences about two brothers. Then write the correct form of *have* or *be* on the lines. The first one has been done for you.

1. Mark and Joseph _____ are _____ brothers.

2. Mark _____ older than Joseph.

3. Joseph _____ 22.

4. Mark _____ 28 years old.

5. Mark _____ a wife and six children.

6. Mark thinks that he _____ lucky because he _____ a wonderful

    family.

7. Joseph _____ not married.

8. Today _____ Joseph's birthday, but Mark forgot.

9. Mark (not) _____ a present for Joseph, but Joseph _____ not

    angry.

10. Joseph knows that his brother _____ many things to do because his family

    _____ so big.

10.2 *Make / Do*

The two verbs *make* and *do* can be a problem because, in some cases, there is almost no difference in meaning between them. The correct verb depends on the other words in the sentence. For example, with the words *bed* and *dishes*, we *make* a bed, but we *do* the dishes.

1. Use *do* as the helping verb in questions and negatives.

    Do you have a car now? What kind of car **did** you buy?

    Mark and Sue **do** not know the answer. John **does** not know the answer.

2. Use *do* when we use it in place of an action verb.

    What are you **doing**? (*doing* = eating, drinking, reading, etc.)

    Colombia exports coffee, and Indonesia **does**, too. (*does* = exports)

    What do you usually **do** in computer lab? (first *do* = helping verb; second *do* = used in place of a verb)

3. Use *do* to talk about general action.

    I'm not **doing** anything.

    Let's **do** something for your birthday.

    The government **did** nothing after the war ended.

4. In general, use *do* to talk about certain kinds of work or activities.

    I **do** my homework.

    I **did** the dishes, and she **did** the laundry.

    Do your best!

5. In general, use *make* to indicate creating or producing something (new).

    He **made** a sandwich.

    The artist **made** an incredible painting.

The following are common expressions with *make* and *do*.

make		do	
make the bed	make a cup of coffee	How are you doing? (greeting)	
make dinner	make a plan	What do you do? (occupation)	
make money	make arrangements	How do you do? (greeting when first meeting)	
make a living	make a telephone call		
make a mistake		do work	do badly
make a profit	make noise	do the laundry	do well
make a promise	make an effort	do homework	do housework
make a difference	make a speech	do something over	do the ironing
make an agreement	make sense	do a favor	do the dishes
make a decision	make progress	do your (my, his, etc.) best	do an exercise
make a mess	make up your mind		do exercise
make an attempt	make a (good) impression	do a job	do an assignment
make a suggestion		do a chore	
make an excuse	make up	do business	do an experiment
make an exception	make a choice	do a favor	do a task
make a change	make up an assignment		
make food			

Exercise 3   Fill in the blanks with the correct form of *make* or *do*. The first one has been done for you.

1. ___*make*___ a living

2. _____ a change

3. _____ the ironing

4. _____ food

5. _____ a cup of coffee

6. _____ an exercise

7. _____ an assignment

8. _____ progress

9. _____ a sandwich

10. _____ the bed

11. _____ a mistake

12. _____ a chore

13. _____ money

14. _____ an agreement

15. _____ the laundry

16. _____ a decision

17. _____ a favor

18. _____ a profit

19. _____ a promise

20. _____ your best

21. _____ an exception

22. _____ a mess

23. _____ dinner

24. _____ an attempt

25. _____ a suggestion

26. _____ a plan

27. _____ up an assignment

28. _____ arrangements

29. _____ badly

30. _____ a telephone call

31. _____ work

32. _____ an excuse

33. _____ a favor

34. _____ the dishes

35. _____ a (good) impression

36. _____ well

37. _____ a choice

38. _____ housework

39. _____ an effort

40. _____ exercise

41. _____ a task

42. _____ business

43. _____ a speech

44. _____ up your mind

Exercise 4 Complete each sentence with the correct form of *make* or *do*. The first one has been done for you.

1. _____ Do _____ you live in a house or an apartment now?

2. What kind of truck _____ you buy last year?

3. Last night I _____ the dishes, and she _____ the laundry.

4. Clare _____ not speak French well, so she can't help you translate the letter.

5. I _____ not think that it will _____ a difference if you wait to

   call Susan tomorrow.

6. If your paper is not so good, you can always _____ it over.

7. What _____ you _____ for a living?

8. How _____ you _____?

9. What are you _____ now?

10. Japan exports cars, and Korea _____ , too.

11. I'm not _____ anything now. Let's go to the mall.

12. Something is wrong. My car is _____ a funny noise.

13. Let's _____ something special for your parents' fiftieth anniversary.

14. Joe and Janet _____ not have a car, so they take the bus to work every day.

15. What _____ you usually _____ after you eat dinner?

16. When I get home, I usually _____ my homework right away.

17. How are you _____?

18. Are you _____ your homework now?

19. To me, flying there _____ more sense than driving there.

20. In science class today, we had to _____ a difficult experiment.

Exercise 5 Read this paragraph about household chores. Complete the sentences with *make* or *do*. The first one has been done for you.

Agreeing

Let's _____make_____ an agreement.
           1

If you _____ the dishes,
           2

I will _____ the bed. If you
           3

_____ breakfast every day,
     4

I'll _____ dinner every evening. If you _____ the laundry, I'll
        5   **6**

_____ ironing. We both hate to _____ housework and we both
     7   **8**

hate to _____ food, so I think that this agreement _____ sense.
            9   **10**

Exercise 6 Read this paragraph about a business decision. Then fill in the blanks with the correct form of *make* or *do.* The first one has been done for you.

Banking

Our company uses Washington Bank. We have _____ done _____ business

                                       1

with them for over a decade. At a company meeting yesterday, my boss _____ a

                                      2

suggestion that we switch to First National Bank of Woodland. I am worried that this

is not a good thing to _____ because I've heard some bad things about that bank.

                                3

I am going to _____ some phone calls to some people who _____

                     4   **5**

business with First National to hear about their experiences with that bank. I

_____ not know what else I can _____ to _____

     6   **7**   **8**

this very difficult decision. I'm responsible for this decision, and I certainly

_____ not want to _____ a mistake that might cost our

     9   **10**

company a lot of money. I wish I could ask a coworker to _____ this task.

                                                    11

10.3 *Say / Tell*

Say and *tell* have the same basic meaning. The difference in their uses is in grammar.

1. Use *say* to mean *say* something.

   The book **says** that the accident happened in 1998.

   She **said** that she would be late.

2. Use *tell* to mean *tell* someone something.

   Please **tell** me which pages we have to read for homework.

   Nobody **told** the driver the address.

   I **told** Joseph to call me.

3. Use *say* for direct speech.

> The driver **said**, "I don't know which house is the correct one."

> He **said**, "I love you," and then he died.

You sometimes use *tell* to give a command or instructions if you name the person that the speaker is speaking to.

> The doctor **told** the young man, "Roll up your sleeves for your shot."

4. Use *say* or *tell* for reported speech.

> The teacher **said** that there would be 100 questions on the final exam.

> The teacher **told** us that there would be 100 questions on the final exam.

5. Use *tell* + person + *to* + verb for orders or advice.

> The teacher **told** *the students to write.*

> The recording **told** *me not to hang up.*

> Please **tell** *your father to call me tomorrow.*

> **Tell** *your wife to take the children* to the beach tomorrow.

6. Use *tell* with these expressions:

tell the truth	tell a lie	tell a story
tell a secret	tell (the) time	tell a joke
tell the future	tell the difference	

Avoid this error: *say* + the person. The biggest mistake is "say me" or "say you."

> *Incorrect:*   He ~~said~~ *me* to open the door.

> *Correct:*   He **told** *me* to open the door.

Exercise 7   Complete each sentence with the correct form of *say* or *tell*. The first one has been done for you.

1. She _____said_____, "Please _____tell_____ me what happened at lunch."

2. Some people believe they can _____ the future by looking at your palm.

3. Can you _____ the difference between Pepsi and Coke?

4. If you want me to _____ you how to get to my house, I can do that.

5. Martha is not here yet, but she _____ me to _____ you that she

   would be late.

6. When she entered the room, did anyone _____ anything?

7. Excuse me. Can you _____ me how to _____ this word

   correctly?

8. If you _____ me a secret, you can be sure that I won't _____

anyone.

9. Please don't _____ anything to anyone about this problem. O.K.?

10. The little boy _____ that he is not _____ a lie, but I don't believe

him.

Exercise 8   Read these sentences about two friends. If the underlined part is wrong, write X and make the correction. If it is correct, write C. The first one has been done for you.

____C____   1. Hector <u>told me</u> to call him at his house around noon.

_____   2. When I called my friend Hector's house, his wife Janice <u>said me</u> that he was

not home.

_____   3. Janice <u>said</u> that Hector was on his way to the store to buy some more cat food.

_____   4. Hector never does what he <u>says</u> he is going to do, so I was not surprised to

find out that he was not home.

_____   5. Sometimes I think that the problem is that Hector can't <u>say</u> time.

_____   6. Janice <u>said me</u> that Hector had his cell phone with him.

_____   7. She <u>said</u> that I should call him on his cell phone.

_____   8. An hour later, Hector finally answered his cell phone and <u>told</u>, "Kevin, I'm

sorry that I wasn't home."

_____   9. Hector <u>said me</u> that he was returning from the store.

_____   10. I <u>said him</u> to call me when he got home to make plans to go fishing next

Saturday.

10.4 *To + Verb*

To answer the question *why*, use **to + verb** in two structures:

to + verb	I came to this school **to** *learn* English.
in order to + verb	I came to this school **in order to** *learn* English.

A common mistake is to use *FOR + verb*. This is not correct English.

Incorrect:	I came here ~~for~~ *learn* English.
Incorrect:	Many people are leaving Haiti ~~for~~ *find* a better life.
Correct:	Many people are leaving Haiti **to** *find* a better life.
OR:	Many people are leaving Haiti **in order to** *find* a better life.

Exercise 9 Read these questions. Answer each question in a complete sentence. Use *to* in some sentences and *in order to* in others. The first one has been done for you.

1. Why do people call their friends?

   People call their friends to make plans or talk about problems.

2. Why do teachers give tests?

   _____

3. Why did you go to (name a place) last year?

   _____

4. Why should people vote?

   _____

5. Why are you (are you not) wearing a watch?

   _____

6. Why do you go to the supermarket?

   _____

7. Why do students use a dictionary?

   _____

8. Why do cities have traffic lights?

   _____

9. Why do some plants have thorns?

_____

10. Why does a coach have a whistle?

_____

10.5   *Many / Much*

1. Use **many** to describe count nouns. (See Chapter 3 for a review of count nouns.)

   This bakery offers **many** *choices* for wedding cakes.

2. You can also use *a lot of* with count nouns. In more formal language, we use *a large number of* with count nouns.

   This bakery offers **a lot of** *choices* for wedding cakes.

   This bakery offers **a large number of** *choices* for wedding cakes.

3. In questions, use *how many* with count nouns.

   How many *people* will this wedding cake serve?

4. Use **much** to describe noncount nouns. (See Chapter 3 for a review of noncount nouns.)

   We do not have **much** *time* to finish the project.

5. You can also use *a lot of* with noncount nouns. In more formal language, we use *a great deal of* with noncount nouns.

   We do not have **a lot of** *time* to finish the project.

   We do not have **a great deal of** *time* to finish the project.

6. In questions, use *how much* with noncount nouns.

   How much *time* do we have to finish the project?

Other phrases:

how much money	how much oil	how much time	how much sugar
how much money	how much oil	how much time	how much sugar
a lot of money	a lot of oil	a lot of time	a lot of sugar

It is not common to use *much + noun* in affirmative statements. It is more common to use *much + noun* only in negatives and in questions.

Incorrect:	~~Much~~ oil comes from Venezuela, Iran, and Russia.
Correct:	**A lot of** oil comes from Venezuela, Iran, and Russia.
Correct:	**A great deal of** oil comes from Venezuela, Iran, and Russia.
Incorrect:	Colombia produces ~~much~~ oil.
Correct:	Colombia does not produce **much** oil.

Exercise 10   Write *many* or *much* to complete each phrase. The first one has been done for you.

1. ____much____ money

2. _____ people

3. _____ ideas

4. _____ children

5. _____ opportunities

6. _____ white sugar

7. _____ extra sharp cheese

8. _____ great ideas

9. _____ economic aid

10. _____ love

Exercise 11   Write *a, an, many,* or *much* to complete each phrase. Sometimes two answers are possible. The first one has been done for you. Hint: Use *a* or *an* with a singular noun.

1. ____many____ great historical novels

2. _____ great historical novel

3. _____ outstanding movie

4. _____ outstanding movies

5. _____ international assistance

6. _____ small Japanese automobiles

7. _____ times

8. _____ time

9. _____ sheep

10. _____ chicken

Exercise 12   Read the paragraph about Mexico and Guatemala. If the underlined part is correct, do nothing. If there is a mistake, write a correction above it.

Same / Different

Mexico and Guatemala are two neighboring

countries. Although there are <u>many</u> differences
                                   1

between the two, they are similar in <u>a lot of</u> ways.
                                        2

One difference is in oil production. Mexico produces

<u>much</u> oil, but Guatemala does not produce <u>a lot of</u> oil. In fact, oil is a very
  3   **4**

(continued)

important export for Mexico's economy. One similarity is in tourism. Both countries

have a very strong tourist industry because of their ancient ruins. <u>Many</u> tourists visit
                                                                      5

Mexico to see the ancient Mayan and Aztec pyramids. Guatemala is smaller than

Mexico, but Guatemala also has <u>much</u> incredible sites for tourists. For example, each
                                6

year thousands of people visit Tikal and Antigua.

10.6 *A Few / A Little*

1. Use **a few** to describe count nouns.

    I can give you **a few** *reasons* to buy this investment.

    Other phrases: a few benefits   a few people   a few times

2. Use **a little** to describe noncount nouns.

    I have **a little** *money* to invest.

    Other phrases: a little food   a little oil   a little time

Exercise 13   Write *a few* or *a little* to complete each phrase. The first one has been done for you.

1. ____*a few*____ people   7. _____ machinery

2. _____ help   8. _____ suitcases

3. _____ work   9. _____ baggage

4. _____ works   10. _____ bank account statements

5. _____ homework   11. _____ scientific thinking

6. _____ machines   12. _____ economic assistance

10.7 Another / Other / Others

The meaning of **another, other,** and **others** is the same: *one more* or *additional.*

> This sandwich is delicious. I'd like **another** one.

> The professor explained three **other** reasons that the war began.

1. **another:** singular adjective or pronoun

   A radio is on the table. **Another** radio is on the shelf. (adjective)

   A radio is on the table. **Another** is on the shelf. (pronoun)

2. **other:** adjective with singular or plural noun

   Sue has two sisters. Ann lives in L.A. Her **other** sister is in London. (singular noun)

   Fay has four sisters. Jill is a nurse. Her three **other** sisters are vets. (plural noun)

3. **others:** plural pronoun

   A few students finished the entire exam. A few **others** finished only one question.

   Some scientists believe in Darwin's theory. **Others** do not accept this idea.

- Do not use *other* when you should use *another*. Do not use *other* as a pronoun; only *another* can be a pronoun.

   Incorrect: This shirt does not fit me. Please give me ~~other~~.

   Correct: This shirt does not fit me. Please give me **another**. (pronoun)

- Do not use *others* when you should use *other*. Do not use *others* as an adjective; only *other* can be an adjective. Remember that adjectives cannot be plural in English.

   Incorrect: Two people are in Room 106. Four ~~others~~ people are in Room 107.

   Correct: Two people are in Room 106. Four **other** people are in Room 107.

Exercise 14   Read these sentences about a health class. In each sentence, if the underlined word is correct, write C on the line. If it is incorrect, write X and correct the mistake. The first one has been done for you.

_____C_____ 1. I like our health class because we study the

nutritional value of different kinds of foods.

Another reason that I like the class is that

sometimes we get to taste the foods that we are

studying about.

_____ 2. Our book has a whole chapter on common picnic foods. I also saw that there

are <u>others</u> chapters with information about cooking different kinds of meat,

vegetables, and desserts.

_____ 3. This week's lesson is about common picnic foods. In lessons from <u>other</u> weeks,

we learned about pasta dishes, rice dishes, and corn dishes.

_____ 4. Yesterday we studied a recipe for potato salad that uses white onions. I have

<u>other</u> recipe that uses green onions.

_____ 5. Some people like the taste of white onions. <u>Others</u> prefer the taste of green

onions.

_____ 6. Some people don't like potato salad because of the onions. <u>Other</u> reason that

they don't like potato salad is because of the mayonnaise.

_____ 7. The main ingredient of course is potatoes. <u>Other</u> necessary ingredients include

mayonnaise and eggs.

_____ 8. All fifteen students in my class had to follow the recipe to make potato salad.

Twelve students' potato salad creations were delicious. Two <u>others</u> students

had some problems when they were boiling the potatoes, and one student

could not follow the recipe at all.

10.8 Too / Very

The meanings of **too** and **very** are similar, but they are not the same.

1. *Very* means *more*. Use *very* before adjectives or adverbs.

   very + adjective: very happy, very difficult, very interesting, very interested

   very + adverb: very much, very carefully, very slowly, very well

2. *Too* means *extremely*. Use *too* before adjectives or adverbs.

   too + adjective: too happy, too difficult, too interesting, too interested

   too + adverb: too much, too carefully, too slowly, too well

3. *Too* and *very* mean *a lot*, but *too* means that something (an action) is not possible.

   I would like to play tennis, but I'm **very** tired. (I might play tennis.)

   I would like to play tennis, but I'm **too** tired. (I will not play tennis now.)

   This book is **very** difficult. (I may be able to understand it.)

   This book is **too** difficult. (I cannot understand it.)

Do not use *too* when you want to say *very* or *extremely*.

   Incorrect: The science exam was ~~too~~ easy. (For what? This is an illogical sentence.)

   Correct: The science exam was **very** easy.

   OR: The science exam was **extremely** easy.

Exercise 15   Read the sentences about a history class. Underline the correct word in parentheses in each sentence. The first one has been done for you.

1. My favorite subject is history. I like it (<u>very,</u> too) much.

2. My history class is at 8:00 a.m. on Monday and Wednesday. I wanted to get into a history class at 1:00 p.m., but there were (very, too) many people in that section already.

3. In my history class, our professor gives us a lot of assignments. Some students think that we have (very, too) many assignments, but I think the amount is just right.

4. I like the class, but the book is (very, too) difficult for some students to read.

5. The professor is a (very, too) good teacher.

6. His lectures are always (very, too) interesting.

Exercise 16   Write four pairs of sentences with *very* and *too*. The first one has been done for you.

1. a. That movie is very long, but I watched it.

   b. That movie is too long, so I didn't watch it.

2. a. _____

   b. _____

3. a. _____

   b. _____

4. a. _____

   b. _____

10.9   Pronouns, Possessive Adjectives, and Possessive Pronouns

It is easy to confuse words such as *me* and *my* or *he*, *him*, and *his*. Here is a list of common subject and object pronouns, possessive adjectives, and possessive pronouns.

Subject Pronouns	Object Pronouns	Possessive Adjectives	Possessive Pronouns
I	me	my	mine
you	you	your	yours
he	him	his	his
she	her	her	hers
it	it	its	——
we	us	our	ours
they	them	their	theirs

1. Subject pronouns

   I am a computer programmer. (subject of the sentence)

2. Object pronouns

   My supervisor congratulated **me** for my good work. (direct object)

   My supervisor was in the meeting with **me**. (object of preposition)

3. Possessive adjectives

   My supervisor was in the meeting with me. (describes *supervisor*)

4. Possessive pronouns

   Your score is 87, but **mine** is only 72. (replaces a possessive adjective + noun: *my score*)

- Do not use a pronoun when you should use a possessive adjective.

    Incorrect: The doctor has **she** books in her car.

    Correct: The doctor has **her** books in her car.

- Do not use a subject pronoun when you should use an object pronoun (or the reverse).

    Incorrect: The teacher gave a study sheet to **we** to study for tomorrow's test.
    (subject pronoun)

    Correct: The teacher gave the diskettes to **us** to study for tomorrow's test.
    (object pronoun)

- Do not forget the subject.

    Incorrect: Today is June 12. Is my birthday.

    Correct: Today is June 12. **It** is my birthday.

    Incorrect: Bolivia and Brazil are beautiful countries. Have many tourist sites.

    Correct: Bolivia and Brazil are beautiful countries. **They** have many tourist sites.

- Do not confuse *he* and *she*.

    Incorrect: Ronald Reagan was the 40th U.S. president. **She** was born in California.

    Correct: Ronald Reagan was the 40th U.S. president. **He** was born in California.

Exercise 17   Read this e-mail about a job application that had some problems. For each numbered item, underline the correct word in parentheses. The first one has been done for you.

```
To: Mike Smith

From: Joshua Brooks

Subject: Application form problems

Dear Mike,

    (I, Me, My, Mine) am sending (you, your, yours) this e-mail
          1                               2

because there is a problem with (you, your, yours) application
                                              3

for the supervising job at (we, us, our, ours) company. In (you,
                                      4

your, yours) application, (you, your, yours) forgot to fill out
     5                            6

a few items in the last section. This section asks for certain
```

(continued)

information about (you, your, yours) education. I remember from
7

our phone conversation that (you, your, yours) have a bachelor's
8

degree, but (you, your, yours) did not write down (you, your,
9   10

yours) graduation year. In the section that asks for contact

information, (you, your, yours) e-mail address is there, but I
11

do not see (you, your, yours) telephone number. Can
12

(you, your, yours) please send it to me as soon as possible? In
13

addition, (you, your, yours) didn't list any of (you, your, yours)
14   15

references. Who is (you, your, yours) current employer? Do
16

(you, your, yours) have a phone number for the company? Do (you,
17

your, yours) carry it with (you, your, yours) during the day?
18   19

Mike, (we, us, our, ours) have (you, your, yours)
20   21

application, but (we, us, our, ours) need all of the information
22

by (we, us, our, ours) official deadline. (It is, Is, Its) next
23   24

Monday, and (I, me, my, mine) hope (you, your, yours) can provide
25   26

the information by that date.

(I, Me, My, Mine) look forward to hearing from
27

(you, your, yours). If (you, your, yours) have any questions,
28   29

(continued)

```
(you, your, yours) can e-mail (I, me, my, mine) or (you, your, yours)
        30                              31                      32

can call (I, me, my, mine) cell at 555-9292.
                 33

Many thanks,

Joshua Brooks
```

10.10   Do Not Begin Sentences with *and / but / so / or*

In speaking, we sometimes begin a sentence with a conjunction (joining word) such as **and, but, so,** or **or.** However, in formal or academic writing, it is not correct to begin a sentence with a conjunction.

Conversation:	Kevin played tennis yesterday. **So** he was really tired.
Writing:	Kevin played tennis yesterday, **so** he was really tired.

Conversation:	Kevin played tennis yesterday. **But** he did not play this morning.
Writing:	Kevin played tennis yesterday, **but** he did not play this morning.

Remember to put a comma between the independent clauses in a compound sentence (see Chapter 9).

Exercise 18   Find and correct the four errors with conjunctions in this paragraph about country names.

Name Changes for Countries

Most countries have had the same names for a

long time, but a few countries have new names. Their

names were changed for historical reasons. Or they were

changed for political reasons. On a current world map,

you can see the country of Myanmar in southeast Asia.

Today we call this country Myanmar. But for many years, it was called Burma. Next

(continued)

to Myanmar is the country of Thailand. For a long time, this country was called

Siam. But now it is called Thailand. South of Thailand are Malaysia and Singapore.

These two countries are completely separate now. For a few years, Singapore and

Malaysia were one country. But in 1963, they decided to separate into two countries.

■ GUIDED WRITING

Exercise 19 Read the paragraph below. Rewrite it by making the eleven changes listed. Careful: You may have to make other changes.

1. Change *very* to *extremely*.

2. The word *thing* is too vague. Change *thing* to *task*.

3. Take out all contractions. In writing, you should write out all of the words.

4. Change *difficulty* to *problems*.

5. Add another simple example after *cat*. Use the connector *or*.

6. Begin the fifth sentence with the phrase *for example* (Hint: add appropriate punctuation.)

7. Connect the first two sentences that discuss consonants with the word *because*.

8. Connect the two sentences about the letter *c* with an appropriate connector.

9. Change the word *problem* to *mistake*. (Hint: This will also require one more change.)

10. Connect the two sentences about the word *straight* with an appropriate connector.

11. Connect the last two sentences with the connector *so*.

English Spelling

Spelling in English is a very difficult thing. Students don't have much difficulty with small words such as *cat*. Longer words can be especially tricky. For some people, vowels are the big problem. The sound of long E can be spelled *ee* as in *beet, ea* as in *each*, or *eo* as in *people*. For other people, consonants cause headaches. One consonant can be pronounced two different ways. Sometimes the letter *c* sounds like *k* as in *cool*. Other times it sounds like *s* as in *race*. Another spelling problem that many people have occurs with silent letters. The word *straight* has eight letters. Three of the letters are silent. English spelling isn't easy. It is not surprising that so many people cannot spell well.

(continued)

_____

_____

_____

_____

_____

_____

_____

_____

_____

_____

_____

_____

_____

_____

_____

_____

■ **CHAPTER QUIZ**

Exercise 20   **Part 1: Synthesis.** Circle the letter of the correct answer.

1. Some customers did not like the store's new plan, but many _____ people supported it fully.

    A. other   C. of other

    B. others   D. of others

2. I believe that it is very useful for all of us to _____ a discussion about any change in the law about owning a gun.

    A. make   C. have

    B. say   D. be

3. Look at this meal! This meat dish in particular is _____ delicious. Can you tell us how you prepared it? What ingredients did you use?

    A. certain   C. very

    B. too   D. extreme

4. Is Paolo leaving now? Does he _____?

    A. have his umbrella with him   C. have him umbrella with his

    B. has his umbrella with him   D. has him umbrella with his

5. High school athletes dream of becoming professionals. _____ practice hard, they may realize this dream.

    A. They   C. And if they

    B. So they   D. If they

6. I applied for that job _____ more money.

    A. to earn   C. for earn

    B. to earning   D. for earning

Part 2: Error Correction. One of the four underlined words or phrases is not correct. Circle the letter of the error and correct it in the space provided.

7. At the press conference yesterday, the spokesperson for the company said that all of
        A   **B**
the information on the company website has right. _____
    C   **D**

8. I think that we should rent a car to drive there. To me, renting a car has more sense
             A   **B**   **C**   **D**
than driving our own car there. _____

9. When we talked to the little boys, he told us that Joshua is not telling a lie, but I don't
    A   **B**   **C**   **D**
believe him. _____

10. My aunt does not eat many kind of vegetables, but she often eats salad with carrots
      A   **B**   **C**
and other root vegetables. _____
    D

■ ORIGINAL WRITING

Exercise 21   On a separate sheet of paper, write an original paragraph (eight to fifteen sentences) about something funny or strange that happened because someone made a simple mistake. Tell what happened and why it was funny. Give details about the event. When was it? Where did it take place? Why did it happen? Use at least five of the following in your writing: *make / do, say / tell, be right, be wrong, many / much, a few / a little, and / but / so.* Underline your uses of these words.

Appendixes

1. Irregular Verb Forms
2. Capitalization
3. Punctuation

1   Irregular Verb Forms

Simple	Past	Past Participle	Simple	Past	Past Participle
be	was, were	been	fall	fell	fallen
beat	beat	beaten	feed	fed	fed
become	became	become	feel	felt	felt
begin	began	begun	fight	fought	fought
bend	bent	bent	find	found	found
bite	bit	bitten	flee	fled	fled
bleed	bled	bled	fly	flew	flown
blow	blew	blown	forget	forgot	forgotten
break	broke	broken	freeze	froze	frozen
bring	brought	brought	get	got	gotten
build	built	built	give	gave	given
buy	bought	bought	go	went	gone
catch	caught	caught	grow	grew	grown
choose	chose	chosen	have	had	had
come	came	come	hear	heard	heard
cost	cost	cost	hide	hid	hidden
cut	cut	cut	hold	held	held
deal	dealt	dealt	hurt	hurt	hurt
dig	dug	dug	keep	kept	kept
do	did	done	know	knew	known
draw	drew	drawn	lead	led	led
drink	drank	drunk	leave	left	left
drive	drove	driven	lend	lent	lent
eat	ate	eaten	let	let	let

(continued)

Simple	Past	Past Participle	Simple	Past	Past Participle
lie	lay	lain	sing	sang	sung
lose	lost	lost	sink	sank	sunk
make	made	made	sit	sat	sat
mean	meant	meant	sleep	slept	slept
meet	met	met	speak	spoke	spoken
pay	paid	paid	spend	spent	spent
put	put	put	stand	stood	stood
quit	quit	quit	steal	stole	stolen
read	read	read	sweep	swept	swept
ride	rode	ridden	swim	swam	swum
ring	rang	rung	take	took	taken
rise	rose	risen	teach	taught	taught
run	ran	run	tear	tore	torn
say	said	said	tell	told	told
see	saw	seen	think	thought	thought
sell	sold	sold	throw	threw	thrown
send	sent	sent	wake	woke	woken
set	set	set	wear	wore	worn
shoot	shot	shot	understand	understood	understood
show	showed	shown	win	won	won
shrink	shrank	shrunk	write	wrote	written
shut	shut	shut			

2   Capitalization

2.1   Basic Capitalization Rules

1. Always capitalize <u>the first word of a sentence</u>.

   Today is not Sunday.

   It is not Saturday either.

   Do you know today's date?

2. Always capitalize the word *I* no matter where it is in a sentence.

   John brought the dessert, and **I** brought some drinks.

   I want some tea.

   My brothers, sisters, and **I** all went to the same college.

3. Capitalize proper nouns—the names of specific people, places, or things.

   Mr. Lee parked his **Toyota** in front of the **Hilton.**

The **Statue of Liberty** is located on **Liberty Island** in **New York.**

There is a huge building on the island that is to the west of the city.

4. In a title, some words begin with a capital letter and some words do not.

Living in Fear	**Romeo and Juliet**	**Harry Potter and the Deathly Hallows**
The King and I	**Three Men and a Baby**	**Love at First Sight**

The rules for capitalizing titles are easy:

- Always capitalize the first letter of a title.

- If the title has more than one word, capitalize all the words that have meaning (content words).

- Do not capitalize small (function) words like *a, the, in, with, on, for, to, above, and, or* (unless they are the first word, in which case they are capitalized).

2.2 *Capitalization Practice*

Practice 1   Circle the words that have capitalization errors. Make the corrections.

1. the last day to sign up for the trip to miami is this Thursday.

2. does jill live in west bay apartments, too?

3. the flight to new york left late saturday night and arrived early sunday morning.

4. My Sister has two daughters. Their names are rachel and rosalyn.

5. if mercedes cars weren't so expensive, i think i'd buy one.

Practice 2   Complete these statements. Be sure to use correct capitalization.

1. USA stands for the United _____ of _____ .

2. The first month of the year is _____ .

3. _____ is the capital of Japan.

4. One of the most popular brands of jeans is _____ .

5. President Kennedy's first name was _____ . His wife's first name was

_____ .

6. Much of Europe was destroyed in _____ (1939–45).

7. All over the world you can see the large golden M that belongs to the most popular

fast-food restaurant in the world, _____ .

8. Beijing is the largest city in _____ .

9. The winter months are _____ , _____ , and _____ .

10. The last movie that I saw was _____ .

Practice 3 Read the following titles. Rewrite them with correct capitalization.

1. my favorite food _____

2. living in Miami _____

3. the best restaurant in town _____

4. mr. smith's new car _____

5. a new trend in Hollywood _____

6. why i left California _____

7. my side of the mountain _____

8. no more room for a friend _____

Practice 4 Read the following paragraph that a student wrote. Circle the capitalization errors and make corrections above the errors.

A visit to cuba

according to an article in last week's issue of newsweek, the prime minister of

canada will visit cuba soon in order to establish better economic ties between the

two countries. because the united states does not have good relations with cuba,

canada's recent decision may result in problems between washington and ottawa. in

a recent interview, the canadian prime minister indicated that his country was ready

to reestablish some sort of cooperation with cuba and that canada would do so as

quickly as possible. there is no doubt that this new development will be discussed at

the opening session of congress next tuesday.

Practice 5   Read the following paragraph. Circle the capitalization errors and make corrections above them.

---

crossing the atlantic from atlanta

It used to be difficult to travel directly from atlanta to europe, but this is

certainly not the case nowadays. british airways offers several daily flights to london.

Lufthansa, the national airline of germany, offers flights every day to frankfurt

and twice a week to berlin. other european air carriers that offer direct flights from

atlanta to europe are klm of the netherlands, sabena of belgium, and air france.

however, the airline with the largest number of direct flights to any european city

is not a european airline. delta airlines, which is the second largest airline in the

united states, offers seventeen flights a day to twelve european cities, including paris,

london, frankfurt, zurich, rome, and athens.

Practice 6   Read the following paragraph. Circle the capitalization errors and make corrections above them.

---

my beginnings in foreign languages

I have always loved foreign languages. When I was in tenth grade, I took my first

foreign language class. It was french I. My teacher was named mrs. demontluzin. She

was a wonderful teacher who inspired me to develop my interest in foreign languages.

Before I finished high school, I took a second year of french and one year of spanish.

(continued)

I wish my high school had offered latin or greek, but the small size of the school

prevented this. Over the years since I graduated from high school, I have lived and

worked abroad. I studied arabic when I lived in saudi arabia, japanese in japan, and

malay in malaysia. Two years ago, I took a german class in the united states. Because of

recent travels to uzbekistan and kyrgyzstan, which are two republics from the former

soviet union, I have a strong desire to study russian. I hope that my love of learning

foreign languages will continue.

3 Punctuation

3.1 End Punctuation

Three main kinds of punctuation occur at the end of an English sentence. You need to
know how to use all three of them correctly.

1. **period (.)** A period is used at the end of a declarative sentence.

    This is a declarative sentence.

    This is not a question.

    All three of these sentences end with a period.

2. **question mark (?)** A question mark is used at the end of a question.

    Is this idea difficult?

    Is it hard to remember the name of this mark?

    How many questions are in this group?

3. **exclamation point (!)** An exclamation point is used at the end of an exclamation.
    It is less common than the other two marks.

    I can't believe you think this is difficult!

    This is the best writing book in the world!

    Now I understand all of these examples!

Practice 1 Add the correct end punctuation.

1. This examination consists of fifty items

2. Read each item carefully to see if you think it is true or false

3. Write T or F on the line to indicate your answer

4. Does anyone have any questions before we start the test

5. You may begin now

Practice 2 Look at an article in any newspaper or magazine. Circle every end punctuation. Then answer these questions.

1. How many final periods are there? _____ (or _____ %)

2. How many final question marks are there? _____ (or _____ %)

3. How many final exclamation points are there? _____ (or _____ %)

4. What is the total number of sentences? _____

Use this last number to calculate the percentages for each of the categories. Does the period occur most often?

3.2 Commas

The comma has several different functions in English. Here are some of the most common ones.

1. A comma separates a list of three or more things. There should be a comma between the items in a list. Do not use a comma between only two items.

    He has lived in Russia and China.

    He has traveled in Brazil, Canada, and Sweden.

    Russia, China, Brazil, Canada, and Sweden are large countries.

2. A comma separates two sentences when there is a combining word (coordinating conjunction) such as *and, but, or, so, for, nor,* or *yet*. The easy way to remember these is FANBOYS (*for, and, nor, but, or, yet, so*). The three most important combining words for this book are *and, but,* and *so*.

    Sammy bought the cake, **and** Paul paid for the ice cream.

    Six people took the course, **but** only five passed the final exam.

    Students may submit their applications by mail, **so** it is not necessary for them to drive to the university to apply.

Note: In general, do not use a comma before *because* or *although*.

    Only five students passed the exam **because** it was very difficult.

    One student scored 97 **although** the exam was very difficult.

3. A comma is used to separate an introductory word or phrase from the rest of the sentence.

> In conclusion, doctors are advising people to take more vitamins.

> First, you will need a pencil.

> Because of the heavy rains, many of the roads were flooded.

> Finally, add the sugar to the batter.

4. A comma is used to mark an appositive. An appositive is a word or group of words that renames a noun. An appositive provides additional information about the noun.

> Washington, the first president of this country, was a clever military leader.
> SUBJ (noun)   APPOSITIVE

In this sentence, the phrase *the first president of this country* is an appositive. This phrase renames or explains the noun *Washington*.

5. A comma is sometimes used with adjective clauses. An adjective clause usually begins with a relative pronoun (*who, that, which, whom, whose, whoever, whomever*). We use a comma when the information in the clause is unnecessary or extra. (This is also called nonrestrictive.)

> The book **that is on the teacher's desk** is the main book for this class.

Here when you say "the book," the reader cannot understand which book you are talking about, so the information in the adjective clause is necessary. In this case, we do not use commas.

> *History of California*, **which is on the teacher's desk,** is the main book for this class.

Here you have the exact name of the book, so the information in the adjective clause is not necessary to help the reader identify the book. In this case, you must use commas to show that the information is extra.

Practice 3   Add commas as needed in these sentences. Some sentences may be correct, and others may need more than one comma.

1. For the past fifteen years Mary Parker has been both the director and producer of all the plays at this theater.

2. Despite all the problems we had on our vacation we managed to have a good time.

3. I believe the best countries to visit in Africa are Senegal Tunisia and Ghana.

4. She believes the best countries to visit in Africa are Senegal and Tunisia.

5. The third step in this process is to grate the carrots and the potatoes.

6. Third grate the carrots and the potatoes.

7. Blue green and red are strong colors. For this reason they are not appropriate for a living room wall.

8. Without anyone to teach foreign language classes next year the school will be unable

   to offer French Spanish or German.

Practice 4   This practice is more difficult. Add commas as needed in these sentences. Some sentences may be correct, and others may need more than one comma.

1. The NEQ 7000, the very latest computer from Electron Technologies, is not selling

   very well.

2. The job interview is for a position at Mills Trust Company, *that* which is the largest

   company in this area.

C 3. The job interview is for a position at a large company that has over 1,000 employees in

   this area.

4. Kevin's birthday is January 18th, which is the same day that Laura and Greg have their

   birthdays.

5. Martina Navratilova, whom most tennis fans refer to only as "Martina," dominated

   women's tennis for years.

6. My brother who lives in Miami has two children. (I have several brothers.)

7. My brother, who lives in Miami, has two children. (I have only one brother.)

8. This flight is leaving for La Paz, which is the first of three stops that the plane will make.

9. No one knows the name of the person who will take over the committee in January,

   so there have been many rumors about this.

10. Bank of Nova Scotia, the most recent bank to open a branch here in Armyville, has tried

    to establish a branch here for years but they just did so this month.

11. On the right side of the living room an antique radio sits on top of a glass table that

    also has a flower pot, a photo of a baby, and a magazine.

12. In Louisiana food is spicy because people there cook with a lot of onions, peppers,

    and seasonings.

3.3   *Apostrophes*

Apostrophes have two basic uses in English. They indicate either a contraction or a possession.

Contractions: Use an apostrophe in a contraction in place of the letter or letters that have been deleted.

> he's (he is OR he has), they're (they are), I've (I have), we'd (we would OR we had)

Possession: Use an apostrophe to indicate possession. Add an apostrophe and the letter s after the word. If a plural word already ends in s, then just add the apostrophe.

> Lincoln's term in office
>
> Mrs. Popkes's three daughters
>
> Yesterday's paper
>
> The boy's books   (= one boy has some books)
>
> The boys' books   (= several boys have one or more books)

Practice 5   Correct the apostrophe errors in these sentences.

1. Im going to Victors birthday party on Saturday.

2. The Smiths house is right next to the Wilsons house.

3. Hardly anyone remembers Roosevelts drastic action in the early part of last century.

4. It goes without saying that wed be better off without atomic weapons in this world.

5. The reasons that were given for the childrens bad behavior were unbelievable.

3.4   *Editing for Errors*

Practice 6   Find the fifteen punctuation errors in this paragraph and make corrections.

Deserts

Deserts are some of the most interesting places on earth A desert is not just a dry

area It is an area that receives less than ten inches of rainfall a year About one-fifth

of the earth is composed of deserts Although many people believe that deserts are

nothing but hills of sand this is not true In reality deserts have large rocks mountains

canyons and even lakes For instance only about ten percent of the Sahara Desert the

largest desert on the earth is sand

Practice 7   Find the fifteen punctuation errors in this paragraph and make corrections.

Tennis

Of all the sports in the world my favorite is tennis I learned how to play tennis when I was fifteen years old. My father taught me how to play and then my brother and I practiced almost every day before school. We practiced in the early morning, because the weather was not too hot I like tennis for a number of reasons. First it is good exercise. Second it is a lot of fun. Third, it is a combination of physical, and mental ability. In fact tennis reminds me of chess. Both games require you to think, and then act. Now tennis is an international sport, and we see that the top players, are from Argentina Russia Australia, and the United States. Do you like what you are reading. If so then I recommend that you start playing tennis.

Index

Top 10   978-0-6184-8105-7
Top 20   978-0-6187-8967-2

elt.heinle.com/Top 10

Heinle International Contact Information

United States
20 Channel Center St.
Boston, MA 02210-1202
United States
Tel: 617-289-7700
Fax: 617-289-7844

Australia / New Zealand
Tel: 61-(0)3-9685-4111
Fax: 61-(0)3-9685-4199

Brazil
Tel: (55 11) 3665-9931
Fax: (55 11) 3665-9901

Canada
Tel: 416-752-9448
Fax: 416-750-8102

China
Tel: 86-10-8286-2095
Fax: 86-10-8286-2089

Japan
Tel: 81-3-3511-4390
Fax: 81-3-3511-4391

Korea
Tel: 82-2-322-4926
Fax: 82-2-322-4927

Latin America
Tel: (52 55) 1500-6000
Fax: (52 55) 1500-6019
Toll Free: 01-800-800-3768

Singapore - Regional Headquarters
Tel: 65-6410-1200
Fax: 65-6410-1208

Taiwan
Tel: 886-2-2558-0569
Fax: 886-2-2558-0360

UK / Europe / Middle East / Africa
Tel: 44-20-7067-2667
Fax: 44-20-7067-2600

CPSIA information can be obtained
at www.ICGtesting.com
Printed in the USA
FFOW03n0745300315
12234FF

9 780618 481057